CW00417476

Mills, Moors and Luddites

by

Lydia and Colin Speakman

*L*eading *E*dge™
press and publishing

in association with

Supported by the
COUNTRYSIDE
COMMISSION

Published by Leading Edge Press & Publishing Ltd,
The Old Chapel, Burtersett, Hawes, North Yorkshire, DL8 3PB.
☎ (0969) 667566

A CIP Catalogue record for this book is available from the
British Library.

ISBN 0-948135-47-6

Edited by Stan Abbott
Series Editor: Stan Abbott
Sketch maps by John Drew*
Designed by Tim Wright
Colour reprographics by Impression, Leeds
Printed and bound in Great Britain by Ebenezer Baylis and Son
Ltd, Worcester
* The maps which accompany the walks in this book are for guid-
ance only. The publishers strongly recommend that walkers also
carry the relevant Ordnance Survey sheet. The appropriate maps
for the areas covered are:
Landranger series – Sheets 110 and 104; Pathfinder series – 691,
692, 702, 703, 714 and 715.

Illustrations

Barry Wilkinson Picture House Ltd and Kirklees Metropolitan District Council Department of Tourism. Additional photography by the authors.

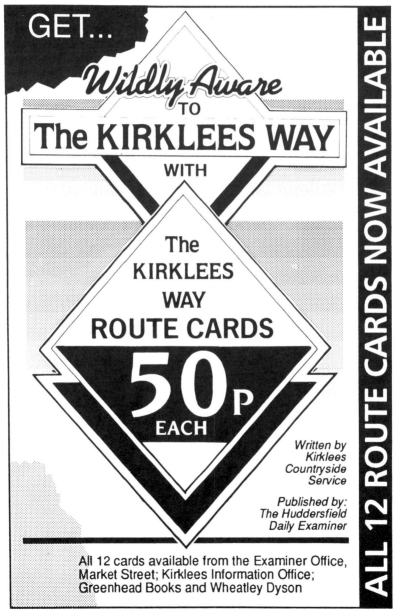

Key to tables

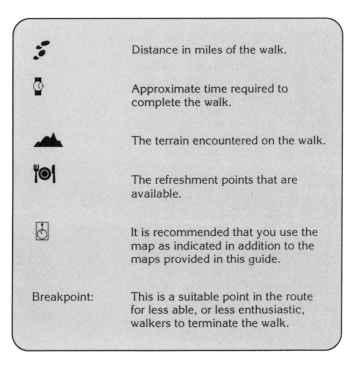

Distance in miles of the walk.

Approximate time required to complete the walk.

The terrain encountered on the walk.

The refreshment points that are available.

It is recommended that you use the map as indicated in addition to the maps provided in this guide.

Breakpoint: This is a suitable point in the route for less able, or less enthusiastic, walkers to terminate the walk.

Foreword

WHILE Kirklees is one of the five metropolitan authorities which make up West Yorkshire, it has both some of the finest undiscovered countryside in England, and an international reputation for its "green activities". In supporting the inexpensive and frequent MetroTrain network in the county, the metropolitan council promotes the use of trains for a healthier environment. Running on lead-free fuel and using less fuel per passenger-mile, MetroTrain can offer the walker and traveller a choice of 15 stations, ranging from the Victorian architectural splendour of Huddersfield to the one-platform halts of Denby Dale and Berry Brow. Coupled with the diverse network of footpaths which radiate from the stations, the railways allow you to get at the "Mills, Moors and Luddite" connections of the Kirklees Countryside.

Kirklees by rail and foot offers an intriguing and rewarding experience for all — so get "Wildly Aware"* of it.

Councillor John Harman
Leader of Kirklees Metropolitan Council

* *"Wildly Aware" is the slogan used by the Kirklees Countryside Unit.*

Contents

(facing page) Sid's Café at Holmfirth

Home from Holmfirth

*London born, Bill Owen who plays Compo in TV's
Last of the Summer Wine has made Kirklees a
second home*

NO-ONE has done more to place Kirklees on the map than those three rascals in TV's *Last of the Summer Wine.*

But for Bill Owen, Compo in the series, the debt is by no means one-way. For his astonishing 21-year stint in the role has awakened in the London born and bred actor a quite remarkable empathy for Yorkshire — a feeling so strong, he says it is as though he had actually been a Yorkshireman in some other life.

Actor Bill Owen, otherwise known as Compo

"Before Last of the Summer Wine, Yorkshire meant no more to me than a series of theatrical dates in places like Leeds, Sheffield or York. Then, suddenly, I was brought up against an entirely different aspect of Yorkshire, since when I have grown to love it far more than my home in London."

"I feel far more at home in Holmfirth than I do in London, almost as if I had been there 'before', and when I get off the train at Wakefield I immediately find myself talking quite naturally in my Yorkshire accent."

"I'm no expert on accents and whatever I do is nothing more than an impression, but the Yorkshire accent seemed to come to me instinctively."

Now Bill is never happier than in his "digs" at Holmfirth, with landlord and landlady, Harry and Ruby Beaumont.

Indeed, so much has Yorkshire's adopted son become part of the area's contemporary culture, that he finds himself involved with all sorts of worthy local causes, such as the canal society and the Holme Valley Trust, which is working on footpaths and environmental improvements in Holmfirth.

There is a seat bearing his name on the town's river walk, a school theatre named after him at Grimethorpe, and he is even the only non-Yorkshireman elected to the Yorkshire Dialect Society. "I am hoping, when I die, to be buried at Holmfirth," he says.

For Bill, this book combines a love of Yorkshire — and especially the Holme Valley — with his other great passion: railways.

He recalls well the heyday of the country railway 50, 60 or 70 years ago, and bemoans the casual disdain with which politicians appear ready to sacrifice such a great asset.

He is a personal friend of Ray Buckton, former General Secretary of the train drivers' union, Aslef, having met him through the Labour Party, and is a powerful advocate of investment in Britain's railways, following the continental example.

In metropolitan areas like Kirklees, of course, our railways have seen significant growth in the last ten years or so. Bill hopes this book may be an inspiration to people who had not thought of the idea of using the train for leisure and pleasure, to help sustain that position in the face of monumental uncertainties. "Use it, or you may find you lose it!"

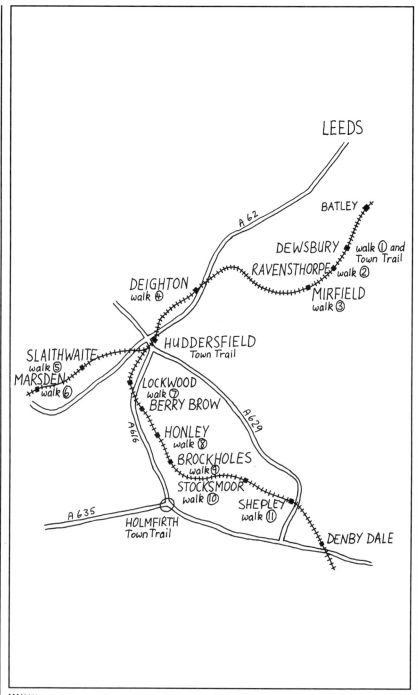

Map showing the location of the walks in this book

Kirklees

KIRKLEES is one of the five Metropolitan districts of West York-shire. It is a landscape of extraordinary contrasts — from the industrial millscape and suburbia of the lower Calder valley, to the desolate open moorland of the Dark Peak and the South Pennines. It takes in lofty reservoirs, deep, green valleys, proud Victorian mill towns and old weaving hamlets where, in tiny little attics, the great textile industry first began which would make the old West Riding, of which Kirklees is a modern part, world famous.

Kirklees by MetroTrain

This book is about all these things. But is also about discovering Kirklees in an environmentally responsible way, using the district's excellent rail network. While cars cause increasing pollution and congestion, noise and visual intrusion, and constant demands for more road space for driving and parking, the local railway network, MetroTrain, makes use of an existing Victorian heritage. Letting the train take the strain also helps the region economically by increasing revenue and reducing deficit, especially at off-peak times.

So, developing public transport for recreation closely mirrors the Kirklees Environment Initiative.

This book offers country and town walks, from a two-mile stroll to a full day's hike in the Peak National Park.

You'll find walks easy to plan — services are hourly on weekdays and two-hourly on Sundays from every railway station in Kirklees. To save money when you travel, there's a choice of either cheap off-peak fares, available weekdays between 9.30am and 3pm, and after 6pm, as well as all-day Saturdays, Sundays and Bank Holidays. And the super-value Metro Day Rover ticket allows you unlimited travel on the MetroTrain network not only at the above times, but without any afternoon restriction, and also on the bus network from your home to the nearest MetroTrain station — one of the best value tickets for ramblers in the UK (for further details phone 0532 457676).

The Moors...

The dominant exposed rock of Kirklees is millstone grit — coarse sandstones laid down in a vast river delta which covered Britain some 280 million years ago. These in turn were raised by the tumultuous earth-movements which compressed and folded these

11

A bleak winter scene of typically exposed moorland heights

sedimentary rocks. Millions of years of erosion by wind, ice and rain, especially during the most recent ice ages which smoothed the hilltops and deepened the valleys, carved the characteristic layers of gritstone, alternating with softer shales or mudstones, to create the shape of the hills as we now see them. The hills tilt up to the west, creating steep escarpments of exposed gritstone towards the Lancashire border, of which Standedge is a notable example. To the east, the hills slope much more gently, towards the Calder and Spen valleys. The contrast can been seen in the fact that Black Hill, Kirklees's highest point, stands 1,098 feet above sea level, but Dewsbury, in the Calder Valley, is a mere 120 feet above sea level.

The landscape of Kirklees is, however, very much a man-made one, shaped and moulded by millennia of farming and, more recently, industrial activity and modern lines of communication. The empty moorlands above the valley heads were once largely covered by forest of birch, alder, hazel, oak and pine that colonised the upland after the last Ice Age. But over the last two thousand years man and his domestic animals, clearing the area for timber, for hunting and farming, have removed the tree cover. Grazing animals, especially sheep on the many ancient, unenclosed Pennine commons, have prevented regeneration, leaving the land vulnerable to leaching by heavy winter rains. Eventually, they have been transformed to rough grazing, heather and bilberry moor, and great, infertile peat hags or cotton grass bogs where only acid-tolerant plants, such as rushes and mosses, will grow. Atmospheric pollution from the burning of coal in homes and power stations added to this process in the 19th and 20th centuries; traffic exhaust pollution adds its share to acid rain today. Many areas, too, have deliberately been left uncultivated because of their value for water catchment. The great, mainly Victorian, reservoirs with their complex system of catchwater drains, is another typical feature of the Kirklees landscape to be experienced on several of these walks.

The mills

People create a landscape. To understand Kirklees is to understand the textile industry and the people who worked in it.

Much of the agricultural land of Kirklees is of poor quality which meant, in mediaeval times, that life was difficult. Poor hay crops from limited areas of valley-bottom land meant that few cattle could be kept. Only tough varieties of sheep could survive the rigours of the moorland climate. For generations before the Industrial Revolution, the Kirklees landscape featured scattered farmsteads along valley sides, inhabited by farmer-clothiers, many of whom lived in "laithe houses", which combined a cottage with weaving chambers above, alongside a "mistal", or cow byre, with a hayloft above. Many families combined farming with the production of coarse, poor-quality cloth from local sheep, known as kersey.

'Millscape' at Slaithwaite

Yeoman clothiers put out small quantities of raw wool or yarn to piece-workers, labouring in their own houses. Families would earn a regular income by selling a small piece of kersey at weekly markets.

During the 15th century cloth-making grew in importance and the area began to draw trade from the West Country. Trains of 20 to 30 animals would carry cloth between trading centres along well-used packhorse roads across the Pennines which can still be seen today. They were often paved with "causey stones" so the trains could cross boggy peat moors.

Entire families were involved in the production of cloth. Wool was sorted into different grades, scoured to remove dirt and grease and then oiled to protect it from the abrasion of the carding and spinning stages. Carding involved the untangling of the matted fleece using wooden brushes studded with iron pins to straighten the fibres into silvers. The silvers were spun into a yarn by either a drop spindle or a spinning wheel. Spinning was mainly carried out by the women and children. Before the yarn was woven it was washed. Baskets of wet yarn were hung by the roadside and anchored in a hole on an outside wall or nearby post. The entire basket was then spun round or "wuzzed" to remove the excess water. Some well-preserved "wuzzing holes" can be found in Golcar, outside the Colne Valley Industrial Museum.

Before weaving, the warp yarn was covered in paste to give it extra strength and prevent it being damaged by the shuttle, and then hung on a beam. The weft yarn was wound on to bobbins and the cloth woven on narrow looms. The cloth which came off the loom was very loosely woven and needed to be "fulled" to make it thick, warm and waterproof. This was often done with lant (stale urine) whose alkaline properties speeded up the felting process. In mediaeval times mechanised fulling mills were gradually introduced, in which water-driven hammers pounded the cloth which was immersed in fuller's earth to remove grease and soap.

The wet cloth was then hung to stretch, from hooks on long rows of parallel posts, known as tenterposts. At one time, every weaving village had its own tenter fields for drying and stretching the newly woven cloth, and larger patches of teasels were also grown. Teasels were used to raise the nap on the cloth which was then cropped with huge shears to produce a smooth finish and disguise the weave.

Kay's development of a flying shuttle in 1732 led to a gradual increase in the production of broadcloth and the decline in the production of kersey. Its spring system meant that weavers did not have to push the shuttle through. By 1780 the flying shuttle was widely adopted and it became possible to earn a living as a handloom weaver. This led to the development of rows of weavers' cottages, built on lower hill slopes or in folds around small courtyards. Many dwellings had extra floors added to create large well-lit loom chambers, giving rise to three and even four-storey blocks lined with long mullion windows. Maximum light was required for the more intricate and delicate weaving of broad cloths. There are some fine examples of weaving cottages in Honley, Netherthong and Golcar, some of which retain their taking-in doors, an independent entrance to the weaving chamber where woollen yarn could be taken in and finished cloth taken out.

During the 18th century there was increased specialisation within the textile industry. Dewsbury concentrated on white cloth and blankets and Huddersfield and surrounding districts specialised in worsteds. Worsted cloth was woven from long wool fibres and finished in such a way as to expose the weave.

Broadcloth production required a much greater degree of fulling than did the smaller coarser kerseys and, with the expansion of woollen manufacturing generally, many more fulling mills were established by master clothiers. Master clothiers also built weaving cottages near to their fulling mills to house the handloom weavers, and these cottages often had communal loom chambers which stretched the entire length of the row.

Mechanisation of the textile industry happened at different paces and at varying times in different regions and branches of the industry. Some of the most important developments of this period were the invention of the spinning jenny, in 1764, by James Hargreaves; the water frame in 1769 by Richard Arkwright; and the spinning mule in 1779 by Samuel Crompton. Richard Arkwright also developed a scribbling engine for carding wool in 1775 which was first introduced in Kirklees, at New Mill in 1780.

The appearance of the early water-powered mills was similar to weaving cottages. Three or four stories high, these early scribbling and spinning mills often had mullioned windows and employed ten or a dozen workers. In the early 19th century the raising of the nap on cloth and cropping was also mechanised through the introduction of gig mills and shearing frames, sparking the Luddite riots. Weaving continued by hand until the mid-19th century.

The introduction of steam power was to have a major impact on the landscape of Kirklees. Mills no longer had to be built near fast flowing streams. Steam power required much larger premises to make full use of the mill engine's capability and provide good return on investment. The new spinning mills were four or five-storey oblong buildings. Alongside them stood handsome engine houses containing the boiler and mill engine, both feeding into a tall chimney. In the early years, steam was only applied to spinning and scribbling, but by the 1860s the use of the power loom had been widely adopted. The weight of power looms and the vibrations caused during their operation meant that they could not be housed in multi-storey buildings. The new weaving sheds were often situated adjacent to existing mills, and there are still many examples around Kirklees, with the characteristic saw-tooth roofs, in which the sloping section normally faces north to provide maximum light, but avoiding the glare of direct sun.

Mechanisation and the growth of markets at home and abroad brought increased specialisation and the development of new products. In the upper Colne valley the mills of Slaithwaite and Marsden concentrated on cotton. The introduction of the Jaquard Loom in Huddersfield in the 1840s enabled the production of patterned cloth and tweeds. Dewsbury, Batley and Cleckheaton became the centre of the heavy woollen industry and the invention of the rag grinding machine in the early 19th century saw the introduction of mungo and shoddy, a material derived from ground-down woollen rags mixed with new wool.

Bigger mills meant many more employees. Men, women and children were employed to keep the mills turning out cloth. It led to a surge in house building around the mills. Valley settlements spread, creating villages like Slaithwaite, Marsden and Milnsbridge, in the Colne valley, and Holmfirth in the Holme valley. Hillside villages developed industrial offshoots in the valley below. Meltham Mills is one such example and Holmebridge, below Holme, is another. The growth in towns led to the building of great stone quarries, not just for the mills and houses, but the entire urban fabric, including cobbled streets and pavements, bridges, public buildings and railway viaducts.

With the expansion of the textile industry came the development of a more sophisticated transport network including, in the mid 18th century, the building of turnpikes all over the Kirklees area. The most famous of these was the Wakefield-Austerland turnpike, built by Blind Jack of Knaresborough in 1759 to link the textile towns of the West Riding and Lancashire. Its route continued from Marsden, crossing the Pennines over Standedge. Blind Jack used a technique to overcome the problem of building across peat moor and bog. Instead of trying to dig down to the bedrock — an impossible task in many areas — he dug a shallow trench and laid bundles of heather along it to absorb and float on the water, beneath a layer of stone for the surface.

The late 18th century was also the era of canal-building, spurred by the growth in trade. The Calder-Hebble Navigation was constructed in 1770 to link Sowerby Bridge to Wakefield, providing easy access to Goole and Hull down the Humber. The canals had an enormous impact on trade. One canal barge could carry the same load as 600 packhorses. Huddersfield was linked to the canal network in 1794, with the construction of the Huddersfield Broad Canal which ran through from the Calder-Hebble navigation at Cooper Bridge, to Aspley Basin in Huddersfield. Between 1793 and 1811 an ambitious project was undertaken, with the construction of the Huddersfield Narrow Canal, a waterway linking Huddersfield and the Upper Colne valley with the Ashton Canal in Cheshire.

The development of the steam locomotive brought the rapid growth of railways from the 1830s onwards, and by 1850 two major lines had been constructed through the district, providing a major impetus to the development of the towns and the textile industry, linking to the ports for both Europe and the expanding British Empire. Exports could now be sent quickly and cheaply to customers all over the world.

Huddersfield was also an early pioneer of the steam tram and eventually had a comprehensive electrified tramway network which ran from the town centre right up the Colne valley to Marsden.

Huddersfield Broad Canal (otherwise known as Sir John Ramsden's Canal) near Deighton

The increasing concentration of population in large centres and the expansion of steam power encouraged the rapid growth of coal mining. Some coal was mined in shallow pits at Meltham and mines at Clayton West. In 1850 there were 40 mines within four miles of Dewsbury town centre, the coal from which was all used to fuel its many mills. Other industries, such as engineering, grew up and, in Huddersfield, came the creation of a chemical dyeing industry, with firms such as Read Holliday and Dan Dawson, now part of ICI.

... and Luddites

The remoteness of the area and the early development of trade and economic diversity created in Kirklees a people of independent spirit. It led to a growth in early Baptism, Methodism and other non-conformist move-

Meltham Parish Church

ments. There are early Quaker Meeting Houses at Wooldale and High Flats. In 1780 John Wesley began his crusade for "vital religion", an evangelical movement which called not simply for the outward observation of religious ritual, but also personal salvation, in pursuit of which Bible reading, regular prayer, abstention, and observation of the Sabbath were signs of grace. Wesley and prominent lay preachers were frequent visitors to the area and what began as a move to revitalise the church, became a break-away movement which left the Church of England and established small chapels. As the movement gained confidence and wealth, larger chapels, such as the Queen Street in Huddersfield and the Zion in Batley, were built. Both could sit more than a thousand people.

Kirklees was also the centre of much Luddite agitation. It was not simply a reaction against new technology but was symbolic of the wide hardship faced by many working people in the years 1811 and 1812, with a bad harvest and depression exacerbated by the naval blockades that accompanied the Napoleonic Wars. The Luddite activity was centred around the croppers, skilled craftsmen who finished the cloth by shearing the raised nap with huge 40lbs shears that were four feet long. Their skill ensured cloth was not damaged and so they were highly paid. In 1800 a shearing frame was developed. It was quite a crude affair comprising simply a pair of shears mounted on a frame and worked by cranks while the cloth was passed underneath by rollers. Many of these shearing frames were made by Enoch Taylor and his brother James, of Marsden. It needed little skill or strength to operate them. In 1811 many masters laid off croppers and turned to the machines to cut costs.

Little is known about the organisation of the Luddites. They had secret signs and pass words and each member swore an oath of secrecy. It was not an anti-government body but rather a systematic campaign for the removal of the new shearing machines. The Luddites wrote to individual manufacturers warning them to cease the use of machinery. The letters were signed "General Lud". Ned Lud was an apprentice at Ansley, near Leicester, who was sacked for smashing knitting frames.

The Kirklees movement began at Longroyd Bridge in John Wood's cropping shop, where his stepson, George Mellor Wood, 22, virtually ran the shop and was believed to be the chief Lud in the area. Also employed there were Thomas Smith and John Walker, later hanged as Luddites, and Benjamin Walker and William Hall who turned informers. William Hall probably brought Luddism to the Spen Valley, where he had originally come from and used to attend regular meetings at the Shears Inn, Hightown. From early 1812 many attacks on shops with new frames took place. They met with little opposition, since small cropping shops were not really able to defend themselves and many of the masters were sympathetic to the croppers' cause. The targets were carefully chosen and there was no wanton destruction. As a result small workshops quickly abandoned their frames.

The authorities were alarmed and a committee of merchants and manufacturers was formed under John Horsfall to seek information. The magistrates, suspecting that the local voluntary militia would be sympathetic to the Luddites, turned to the army. At one point there were more soldiers in the manufacturing districts than Wellington had in the Peninsula War. One man well known for his activities in opposition to the Luddites was Joseph Radcliffe, of Milnsbridge House. His life was frequently threatened and troops were permanently stationed at his house. The Luddite attacks adopted a serious character only when the larger mills determined to keep their frames. An attack on Vickerman's, of Taylor Hill, was successful, but they failed to storm Atkinson's, of Bradley Mills.

The most notorious attack was on Cartwright Mill, at Rawfolds, on the night of April 11/12, 1812. A group of men assembled near the Dumb Steeple, at Cooper Bridge, and marched two-abreast over Hartshead Moor. A few had guns, the rest sticks and stones. Cartwright was well prepared and had his men and five soldiers who had slept in the mill. The mill door was studded with iron and there were spiked rollers on the stairs and tubs of vitriol (sulphuric acid) at the top of the stairs. The Luddites failed to smash the door and there was a brief gun battle outside, in which two of the Luddites were mortally wounded. They died in Robertstown, refusing to the last to give the authorities any information about their fellow Luddites. It is said that they were secretly buried in Hartshead Church with assistance from the then incumbent, one Patrick Brontë.

Two abortive attempts were later made on Cartwright's life. Another prominent opponent of the Luddites was William Horsfall, who owned Ottiwells and Bank Bottom Mill in Marsden, employing 400 men. On April 28, 1812 he was returning from the Cloth Hall in Huddersfield when he was shot on Crosland Moor at the junction of Blackmoorfoot Road and Dryclough Road. William Horsfall was fatally wounded and died a few days later. George Mellor, William Thorpe, Benjamin Walker and Thomas Smith were convicted of his murder, although all of them had alibis. In the trials that followed the attack on Rawfolds Mill and Horsfall's murder, 17 men were hanged and many more were transported. The rest went to Woodsome Hall to swear an oath of allegiance and obtain a free pardon.

As well as being a centre for agitation against the Corn Laws and the Poor Law, Kirklees was also the centre for Chartist agitation in the 1830s and 40s. This nationwide grass roots movement sought to improve the conditions of ordinary men and women by extending the franchise to all working men, through the introduction of a secret ballot and Parliamentary reform. Its demands were encompassed in a six-point charter which was presented to Parliament three times, alongside a petition. The Chartists held a mass meeting and torchlight procession on Hartshead Moor. The Skelmanthorpe Flag, made in 1819 after the Peterloo Massacre, was carried there, amid demands for freedom for all men. As the campaign wore on, the Chartists became increasingly frustrated and violent. This culminated in 1848 with the Plug Plot Riots in which plugs were drawn from steam boilers bringing production to a standstill. In Kirklees the Plug Plots were concentrated around Dewsbury and Cleckheaton.

Kirklees was also the setting for much of the work for factory reform, led by Robert Oastler, the "factory king" who was the estate manager at Fixby Hall, near Huddersfield. He became leader of the movement, publishing pamphlets against the conditions of factory workers, such as the "Manifesto to the working classes of the West Riding". Oastler campaigned to stop child labour in factories and for the movement to shorten the working day to ten hours.

The Huddersfield Line

THE North Trans-Pennine line links the two great cities of Leeds and Manchester via Huddersfield and Dewsbury, and is the busiest and most important railway across the Pennines. Every few minutes the latest Class 158 turbo-diesel Super Sprinters speed effortlessly along its well polished tracks on their way between the great towns and cities of the North of England. The line

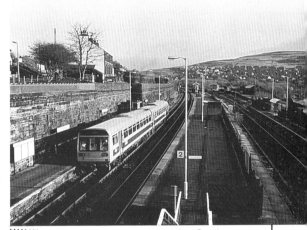

Class 142 Pacer at Marsden Station

travels through the heart of Kirklees from the industrial lowlands around Dewsbury to the dramatic Pennine moors above Marsden.

The first railway across the Pennines was the 61-mile Calder Valley line, built in 1841 by the Manchester and Leeds Railway Company, which become the Lancashire and Yorkshire Railway Company (L&Y) in 1847. George Stephenson designed the line to keep gradients to a minimum and it therefore took a circuitous route, involving a journey of three hours along the Calder Valley. During the planning of the line, there were several public meetings in Huddersfield to urge the Manchester-Leeds railway to pass through the town. One public meeting ended in uproar when a company official announced that the Huddersfield traffic was "not worth stopping the engine for". In 1843 a branch line was proposed to link Huddersfield to the railway at Coopers Bridge, but was strenuously rejected because the route suggested by the company was so close to the valley bottom, it would have been impossible to extend the line beyond Huddersfield.

The building of the Manchester-Leeds line caused a further decline in receipts for the already ailing Huddersfield Narrow Canal. As early as 1825 it had been suggested that the canal should be filled in and the tunnel used for a railway. The canal company refused an offer from the Manchester and Leeds Railway Company, and instead sold out, in 1844, to the Huddersfield and Manchester Railway and Canal Company, which was promoting a line from Cooper Bridge to Stalybridge junction on the Sheffield, Ashton-under-Lyme, and Manchester railway. By 1847 the company had become part of the London North Western Railway (LNWR) network. The line was authorised in Parliament in 1845 and took four years to complete.

It was decided to build the new line parallel to the canal to save construction costs. By following the line of the existing canal tunnel under Standedge, the engineer Thomas Nicholson was able to make much more accurate estimates, as well as making use of the old shafts for excavating the tunnel, and using canal barges in the existing parallel canal tunnel to remove the earth, saving about £70,000. It was, however, an immense feet of engineering and a tribute to the two thousand navvies who worked in appalling conditions to build the tunnel. In all, 150,000lbs of candles were used in the tunnel's construction, at a cost of £3,500. When Standedge tunnel was opened in 1849, it was three miles 66 yards long and became Britain's longest railway tunnel, a record it held until the building of the Severn Tunnel 40 years later. It is still the third longest railway tunnel in England.

At the same time as this tunnel was being constructed, a Leeds, Dewsbury and Manchester Railway was also being promoted. It was authorised on June 30, 1845 to build a line from Leeds to Heaton Lodge junction, at Coopers Bridge, where it would join the Huddersfield and Manchester railway. This line was also operated by the LNWR and the first section, between Huddersfield and Heaton Junction, opened in 1847 and the section to Leeds was completed in 1848.

Apart from Standedge, the line between Leeds and Stalybridge was double-tracked and, as traffic increased, the tunnel became a bottle neck, especially since each train had to be taken through with a pilot engine. Another tunnel was added in 1871 and then a new double-track tunnel — the one still in use today — was added to cope with expanding passenger and freight traffic, in 1894.

Travelling the line — Batley to Marsden

The best way of exploring the Huddersfield line is to begin your journey at Leeds, where local trains call at Cottingley and Morley, then go through Morley Tunnel, to Batley. The rather more leisurely speed of the "local" Pacer gives you more time and opportunity to enjoy the varied scenery than a high speed 156 or 158 Sprinter.

Your local train service might go as far as Huddersfield, or operate to Marsden, or even Manchester Victoria. It is likely to be either a Class 141 or 142 Pacer, one of the first or second generation lightweight diesel railbus vehicles developed by British Rail, in partnership with British Leyland, in the early 1980s to provide a low cost replacement for the aging diesel multiple unit trains, used until then on all West Yorkshire services.

Up to the early 1960s there used to be regular "rhubarb trains" from Morley, from where locally grown rhubarb would be sent by special train to Leeds and on to Kings Cross, to the dining tables of London. From immediately west of Morley Station the line goes through Morley Tunnel, almost two miles long, and into Kirklees.

Batley station once had five through platforms for local services, as well as a bay serving the branch line to Birstall. Just two platforms now survive, all the other lines having been closed and the rest of the station area redeveloped. From Batley, the line crosses a 16-arch viaduct, from where there are magnificent views across to the sandstone escarpments above a valley of densely packed Victorian mills, chapels, chimneys and terraced houses, which merge directly into Dewsbury. The line enters Dewsbury over an impressive viaduct. To the left, as the train slows down into Dewsbury Station, is the striking warehouse of Machells Brothers, manufacturers of shoddy and mungo (see Dewsbury Town Walk).

Dewsbury was once served by three stations owned by the Lancashire and Yorkshire Railway, Great Northern Railway and London and North Western Railway respectively, the last being the only one still in use. This has recently been repainted to show off its fine Victorian cast iron work. Our train leaves Dewsbury following the River Calder before crossing it by a long viaduct. Below the viaduct is the formation of the former L & Y Spen Valley line, which ran from Thornhill to Heckmondwike, Cleckheaton and Low Moor, part of which remained in use as a freight line until the late 1980s. The train now crosses the Calder and Hebble Navigation and continues to Ravensthorpe station. Part of this historic (LNWR) station was recently destroyed by fire.

Immediately beyond Ravensthorpe station is the LNWR junction, where the original Leeds and Dewsbury railway met the line from Horbury and Wakefield, which is mainly used for freight from the huge Horbury sidings, but also carries MetroTrain Huddersfield Line trains from Wakefield. Both lines follow the Calder Valley for the next two and a half miles, soon going alongside a broad curve of the river. Local trains now find themselves using the "slow" line to allow Trans-Pennine express trains to overtake at speed. The line recrosses the Calder River just before the site of the Cleckheaton Junction which linked Huddersfield with the former L & Y line along the Spen Valley to Bradford, via Low Moor. This line closed in 1965.

Mirfield Station, once a large junction, with trains to Wakefield, Bradford and Manchester via the Calder Valley, and served by several canopied platforms, has been rebuilt as an unstaffed halt with MetroTrain bus stop style shelters and an interesting arrangement of staggered platforms on fast and slow lines. To the left are views towards Hopton Woods. Just beyond Mirfield Station, at Heaton Lodge Junction, the lines split.

The central twin tracks form the freight-only Calder Valley line to Sowerby Bridge, while what appear to be two single-track branch lines veer underneath to reform as the main line, curving southwards at Cooper Bridge along the Colne Valley, a tributary of the Calder, to Deighton and Huddersfield. There are plans for passenger services to be restored along the lower Calder Valley, including the reopening of Brighouse and Elland Stations.

Deighton was originally on the Kirkburton branch line, which closed in 1930. The present station was built in 1982 by Metro as a commuter halt. The approach into Huddersfield passes some attractive areas of woodland to the right, then some magnificent views, left, across the town's distinctive millscape as far as Castle Hill and the Jubilee Tower, before your train is rattling across the points and crossing the viaduct into Huddersfield Station. (For a description of the station see the Huddersfield Town Walk).

Most weekday stopping trains to Marsden from Huddersfield come from Wakefield and you will probably have to change trains for the Upper Calder Valley to catch a service to Manchester Victoria. However, Sunday and some peak hour services operate through from Leeds and Batley to Marsden, where they terminate. The train leaves the station by a tunnel and, at Springfield Junction, bears right along a rock cutting which was once the site of a Longwood and Milnsbridge station, now long gone.

The line continues up the Colne valley, over the 20-arch Milnsbridge viaduct, before passing the site of the once extensive Longwood goods yard. Golcar station has long since disappeared, but there are fine views across to this weaving settlement, with its church which seems to dominate the village (see Walk 3). A little further on is Linthwaite and the large six-storey "Titanic" mills on the left, completed in 1911 just after the passenger liner Titanic had sunk. It is said that the mill should have been seven storeys high but someone absconded with the company's money before it was completed. Just before Slaithwaite Station, on your left, are the two huge mill complexes Spa Mill (1906-7), built on the Lancashire cotton spinning mill design, and Globe Mills, a worsted spinning complex, built in 1887. Slaithwaite Station was reopened in 1982, a few yards east of its original site, between two viaducts, its staggered platforms are located at either side of an access road to avoid the need for an expensive footbridge.

The section of line between Slaithwaite and Marsden, through the upper Colne Valley, is perhaps the most dramatically beautiful part of the whole route of the Trans-Pennine railway between Newcastle and Liverpool. Closely following the River Colne and the

Huddersfield Narrow Canal, it overlooks the series of locks and glistening reservoirs which help maintain the canal water level. All around is magnificent, open moorland, crossed by drystone walls, in the foreground scattered farmsteads, isolated groups of weaving cottages, and small stone-built settlements. Ahead is Marsden, lying in a vast basin of hills, its mill chimneys set against a high backcloth of green and brown Pennine moors.

Marsden Station has recently been given a new platform on the loop to allow expresses to overtake local services, and is a pleasant place to terminate your journey and walk half a mile along the canal towpath to Tunnel End Canal and Countryside Centre and the entrance to the Standedge Tunnels, almost 700ft above sea level. On the left is the entrance to the original Nicholson tunnel which, along with the other single bore tunnel, was closed in 1966.

Alternatively you might like to stay on the train for the dramatic ride through Standedge Tunnel, to Greenfield, in the lovely Tame Valley on Greater Manchester's South Pennine fringe.

 Class 158 Trans-Pennine Express entering Tunnel End at Marsden

The Penistone line

THE Penistone line links Huddersfield with Penistone, Barnsley and Sheffield. As well as being a strategic route to the south, it serves numerous small but important settlements in South Kirklees, and also provides an opportunity to discover some delightful Kirklees countryside, either from the comfort of a railway carriage, or on foot from a choice of strategically placed stations. It is also a magnificent piece of Victorian railway engineering, rarely enjoying the easy advantage of a valley, but cutting right across the grain of the South Pennine foothills, over several rivers and their tributaries by a series of splendid viaducts, cuttings, tunnels and embankments.

It was built not as a through line to Sheffield but to link Huddersfield with Penistone Junction and the newly constructed Manchester, Sheffield and Lincoln Railway, which later became part of the Great Central Railway, which ran from Manchester to Sheffield via the Woodhead tunnel and into Sheffield's Victoria Station. Known as the Huddersfield and Sheffield Junction Railway, the line was given Royal Assent on June 30 1845 and opened in 1850, by this time coming under the control of the wealthy Lancashire and Yorkshire Railway Company. Regular passenger services ran between Huddersfield and Penistone Junction, by the 1870s operating through to Sheffield and, by the turn of the century, direct to London's Marylebone Station, via the Great Central Railway.

The eventual closure of the Woodhead line to passengers in 1970, and to freight in 1981, led to a period of great uncertainty before agreements were reached between the South Yorkshire and West Yorkshire Passenger Transport Authorities. This led not only to the re-routeing of trains via Barnsley, but also the reopening of stations at Silkstone, Dodworth and Berry Brow, and much improved frequency of service, including today a direct link to the new Meadowhall Shopping Centre, Sheffield.

A trip along the line —
Huddersfield to Denby Dale and Penistone

Like the local services along the Colne Valley, your Penistone Line train is likely to be provided by a Class 141 or 142 Pacer lightweight diesel railcar.

The excitement of the journey begins from the very moment you leave Huddersfield's magnificent neoclassical station. You plunge into a twin tunnel which runs parallel for a short while with the main

Huddersfield-Manchester line, before diverging at Springwood Junction to cross the Colne valley by the 15-arch Paddock Viaduct. The viaduct crosses the main A62 Manchester Road and provides some superb panoramic, albeit mainly industrial, views across Huddersfield and the Colne Valley, stretching from the mill complexes alongside the canal to the elegant suburbs around Almondbury and below Castle Hill.

A 205-yard tunnel leads to Lockwood station, the first on the branch. Just past the station on the right hand side, once ran the 3½-mile branch line to Meltham, now part of a nature trail. The Meltham branch was opened in 1868 and, as well as stations at Meltham, Healey House and Netherton, there was a halt at Meltham Mills for employees. In 1874 another station opened at Dungeon Woods, below Beaumont Park (see Walk 6) but proved a financial disaster and closed a mere 29 days later; surely one of shortest-lived stations of all time. The branch finally closed to passengers in 1949 but lingered on as a freight branch until April 1965.

The train now eases its way over the magnificent 34-arch Lockwood Viaduct, an impressive structure, 136ft high and 476 yards long. The viaduct is the largest of its kind in the country and was built from stone quarried out of the cutting leading to the next station, Berry Brow.

Berry Brow station is not in its original position. The old station was closed in 1966 but reopened at its present site, nearby in 1989. The old station used to be famous for a sandstone carving by JC Stocks (1886), representing a Barton Wright 0-4-4T locomotive and train, surmounted by a portrait of Thomas Swinburn who worked on the line as an engineer. An earlier carving by Thomas Stocks, of 1866, was destroyed beyond recognition by vandals but the surviving one can now be seen at the Tolson Memorial Museum in Huddersfield. The new station has been skillfully constructed in a narrow cutting and landscaped with evergreens.

Beyond Berry Brow station there are fine views to the left across to Castle Hill and the Jubilee Tower. A full history and description of the tower can be found in Walk 10. From Berry Brow the line travels for a short time above and alongside the Holme valley, soon going through the 228-yard Robin Hood Tunnel, to Honley Station and views across to Honley village on the other side of the valley, with its terraced weaving cottages and distinctive church. The line continues along leafy embankments to Brockholes Station, where the original L & Y buildings are now a private house.

From Brockholes, passengers used to be able to change trains to travel the two-mile branch to Holmfirth. This double-track branch was constructed at the same time as the rest of the line and, although the railway company had permission to extend it up to Holmbridge, the extension was never built. The Holmfirth branch closed to passengers in 1959 and for freight in 1965.

From Brockholes, the line begins to climb on a 1:100 gradient as it enters the 1,631-yard Thurstonland Tunnel. On July 1 1850, on the inaugural journey, with the train overloaded with passengers, the locomotive slipped on the wet rails and stalled in the tunnel. The first few coaches were detached and taken to Stocksmoor Station, leaving the rest of the passengers stranded in the tunnel, waiting for the engine to rescue them.

Beyond Thurstonland Tunnel is a 1 1/2-mile cutting to Stocksmoor Station, which serves a very small community and, although there is a pub, there are few houses nearby. The line then crosses a short embankment, providing brief views, left, across to the 1,084ft high Emley Moor TV mast. Emley Moor mast is the highest structure of its kind in Europe, higher even than the Eiffel Tower. The mast transmits to 4.7 million people in the Yorkshire Television region and replaced an earlier transmitter which collapsed under the weight of ice in 1969.

The train then crosses a wooded valley and goes through Smore cutting, to Shepley. Shepley Station is only three quarters of a mile from Stocksmoor and the old station still survives as a private house, and serves a somewhat larger mill village community.

Not far beyond Shepley is the old Clayton West Junction where trains used to branch off left to Skelmanthorpe and Clayton West. This branch line opened in 1879 and was used to carry coal from pits at Skelmanthorpe, but in later years survived only to take children to a local comprehensive school. The branch finally closed in 1983, but part of it is now the Kirklees Light Railway Company Ltd which is based at Clayton West Station. A 15 inch narrow-gauge steam line runs for approximately two miles (for more information phone 0484 865727).

The 906-yard Cumberworth Tunnel leads to a single-track cutting and Denby Dale Station. Don't forget, if you have a Metro Day Rover, your ticket isn't valid beyond Denby Dale, the last station in West Yorkshire, so if you do decide to travel to Penistone (and it's worth the trip) there is an excess fare to pay. As the line crosses the viaduct, which dominates the little town 112ft below and to the left, you will also see, to the right, a fine mill chimney, weaving sheds and the remains of two stone arches which used to carry the line onto a timber viaduct. In the interests of safety, the viaduct had fire buckets at intervals along its whole length, but because of the vibrations caused by passing trains, these could only be kept half full. The structure partially collapsed in gales in 1847 and, in 1851, Robert Stephenson examined this and other L & Y timber viaducts and reported his "entire conviction of their perfect safety". But, by the 1870s, the viaduct was rotting and it was replaced by the present structure in 1882.

Denby Dale is most famous for its huge meat pies, baked about once every generation. Outside the Pie Hall stands a huge metal dish, now converted into a flower bed, but which once held the enormous 18ft long, 6ft deep Denby Dale pie of 1964. That pie

The Denby Dale Pie of 1964 (picture courtesy of the Huddersfield Examiner*)*

contained 3 tons of beef, 1 1/2 tons of potatoes, and half a ton of gravy and seasoning. The 650 square feet of crust were made from half a ton of flour and half a ton of lard, all baked in a local farmer's newly built milking parlour.

The first pie was baked in 1788 to celebrate George III's (temporary) recovery from madness. Since then, pies have been baked to celebrate events, including the victory over Napoleon, the repeal of the Corn Laws, Queen Victoria's Golden Jubilee and the pie's own 200th anniversary, in 1988. Not all the pies have been successful. In 1887 the filling went bad and smelt so terrible, it had to be buried with quicklime in nearby Toby Woods. At another baking, a stampede almost destroyed the pie and several people were injured. However, pie bakings were always popular and, in 1897, special trains carried 100,000 people from Huddersfield to see the pie, and the station ran out of tickets.

From Denby Dale viaduct, the line continues across a series of embankments, passing between rolling hills, hedgerows and scattered farmsteads, before entering Wellhouse tunnel and continuing across Penistone viaduct. The 29-arch viaduct towers over the Don valley, providing fine views over the town. Towards the end of January 1916 a slight crack was noted in a parapet at the station end of the viaduct. It was examined by an engineer and it was decided there was no cause for anxiety and traffic continued. At 4.07pm on February 3, a train from Huddersfield crossed the viaduct into the station. A few minutes later it was starting to shunt round the curve when the track ahead appeared to bend. The driver and fireman jumped off and ran to the station; the locomotive wasn't so lucky. Two seconds later a pier and two arches collapsed beneath the weight and the engine crashed into the river below. Most of the locomotive ended up as spare parts and scrap, but its chimney became a rather delightful flower pot on Brockholes Station, although sadly it is no longer there.

Penistone Station, now partly a craft centre, still has some of its original Victorian ironwork in place, recalling the days when Penistone was the junction of four busy passenger railways, including the famous Woodhead line across the Pennines to Manchester, and as well as a mineral line to Wath. If you look carefully at the scroll of the ironwork supporting the remains of the canopies on the Huddersfield-bound platform, you'll see the initials of the long vanished Manchester Sheffield and Lincoln Railway, skilfully incorporated into the design.

A walk round Dewsbury

Dewsbury

IN the late 19th century, Dewsbury was the undisputed centre of Yorkshire's Heavy Woollen District, producing blankets, carpets and large quantities of mungo and shoddy. In 1875, three quarters of the world's shoddy trade was carried out in Dewsbury. Shoddy is a loose woven fabric that was once favoured for coat linings and cheap workmen's clothing. Mungo is a much tougher, harder fabric and is made from tailor' clippings to produce a close-knit felt, excellent for army greatcoats. The development of the rag grinding machines in 1813, together with the expansion of steam-powered mills, led to the rapid growth of the town from a population of 4,500 in 1801, to 30,000 in 1900. Dewsbury provided the blankets for both sides of the American Civil War and, in the First World War, the town established a flourishing trade, recycling army clothing from the Western Front. Wormalds and Walkers is still one of the largest blanket producers in Europe.

In the 19th century most of Dewsbury's shoddy and mungo firms were small concerns employing about 12 people. Sorting the rags was skilled work and this was carried out almost exclusively by women who sorted them by colour and grade. The rags were then pulled apart by the grinding machines, known locally as "devils", creating vast amounts of dust. The woollen, and shoddy and mungo mills were powered by steam engines, fired by local coal. In 1850 there were 40 coal pits within three miles of the town centre. The majority were small and shallow, known as day holes because they did not require a shaft, the coal being mined from the surface. In the mid-19th century the lower Calder Valley was full of tall mill chimneys, weaving sheds and densely packed terraced houses, all contributing to the heavy smog that hung over the town, blackening the buildings and pavements with soot.

Today, many of the fine Victorian buildings and warehouses, built from the earnings of 19th century Yorkshire enterprise, have been restored and cleaned and reflect the town's rich industrial heritage. The old warehouses have new roles as offices, night clubs and a vibrant new arts centre. Yet, for the visitor to Dewsbury, the town's chief glory must be the market on Wednesdays and Saturdays when it positively bustles with colour and activity.

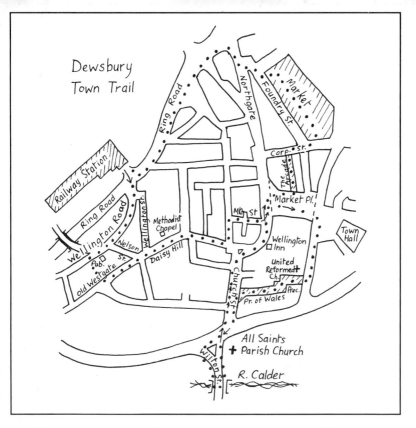

Dewsbury Town Trail

The town trail

🚶 *Begin outside the railway station.*

The station has been recently restored to show off its fine glass canopy and cast iron supports. The station was built in Tudor-style in 1848 by the London and North Western Railway Company to serve the Standedge line, running from Leeds through to Huddersfield and Manchester.

🚶 *Cross over the main Ring Road by the pedestrian crossing to Wellington Street and the old Dewsbury Union. Turn right, but take the next street on the left, which is Wellington Road.*

Wellington Road is lined with ornate warehouses built by the LNWR in Italian Renaissance-style in the 1860s; these handsome buildings reflect the wealth and prosperity of Victorian Dewsbury, which was the European centre of the shoddy trade. Indeed many German and Italian companies sent their agents to live in Dewsbury. Originally some of these warehouses would have been selling houses but would have become warehouses in the 1880s.

Dewsbury town hall

Here, rags were sorted out by colour and grade ready for carbonisation, to remove non-wool material and enable the remainder to be ground down into a material not unlike new wool. This was then mixed with new wool and respun as shoddy and mungo. Today many of the warehouses have been converted into offices and one is now a night club.

🏃 *Continue down Wellington Road, past Nelson Street (also laid out by the railway company), on the left, to the Old Turk pub. Just past the pub go down a cobbled alley and steps into Old Westgate, to the Back Tulip, once called the Dyers Arms (look at the old date stone [1889] above the door). Turn left along Old Westgate continuing down Daisy Hill.*

Daisy Hill, together with the Market Place, was the centre of old Dewsbury. To the left are warehouses and the Methodist Chapel, built in 1846. Methodism was brought to Dewsbury by John Wesley who preached on Dewsbury Moor on the evening of May 26, 1742. The Methodists were to dominate Dewsbury life through their influence within the Liberal Party.

🏃 *Turn left up Union street at the foot of Daisy Hill and then next right down Market Street, turning left at the bottom into Market Place.*

The Market Place has recently been restored and closed to traffic to provide an attractive public space, full of Victorian-style street furniture. This was the site of the original mediaeval market which was granted a charter in 1318. In the 17th century the population of Dewsbury was almost wiped out by the plague and the market closed. It was revived in 1742 when a roundhouse, and later a market cross, were built. There were markets stalls here until 1937. Today the market is held between Foundry Street and Crackenedge Lane.

On the left is the ornate Midland Bank built in the late 19th century. Also worth looking at is the Black Bull pub, on the right, complete with a small bearded devil peering from between the carved stone work. On the right, too, is Barclays Bank, once the West Ridings Union Bank. This building replaced the Royal Hotel which was used as a posting hotel. It was once the scene of Chartist agitation. Most Chartist demonstrations were peaceful but, in 1838, fired by the radical Chartist leader, Fergus O'Connell, a mob of between 5,000 and 7,000 besieged the Dewsbury Poor Law Guardians in the Royal Hotel. In 1842 Dewsbury was once again at the centre of more violent Chartist activity with the Plug Plot riots, in which a rampaging mob halted production by drawing the plugs from the boilers of the steam-powered mills. The mob were not stopped until they reached Cleckheaton, several miles away.

⚲ Cross Market Place to the right, towards the Town Hall.

The Town Hall dominates the Market Place. It was designed by Henry Ashton and George Fox in grand Italianate-style, and built in 1888-89 to mark the town's status as the 'Queen of the Heavy Woollen District'. Outside the Town Hall is the 'Statue of the Good Samaritan', by Ian Judd, erected in 1991 to commemorate the pedestrianisation of the centre of Dewsbury. To the left of the Town Hall is the modern, uninspiring Empire House; this stands on the site of the old mediaeval manor house.

⚲ Turn right into Long Causeway, past the small park which was once the site of the Lancashire and Yorkshire Railway Central Station, opened in 1867 and closed in 1930. A little further on, on the left, is the fine ornate façade of the United Reformed Church which has a particularly impressive doorway. Turn right into and through the Princess of Wales Shopping Precinct. At the Church Street exit, cross at the crossing and turn left to the Ring Road (Vicarage Road) and cross a second pedestrian crossing to Dewsbury Parish Church, All Saints.

It is said that St Paulinus preached at Dewsbury to the Saxon inhabitants in 627AD. He was on his way north from Kent with Queen Bertha, for her marriage to King Edwin of Northumbria, and baptised converts in the River Calder. It is not known how accurate this story is and some scholars suggest that Dewsbury's links with the saint may have arisen from the monastery of Abbot Thrydwulf, which later kept Paulinus's altar safe for the monks fleeing Northumbria. It is, however, undisputed that, in mediaeval times, Dewsbury was the centre of an enormous parish, receiving tithes from an area which stretched 400 square miles from Wakefield to the Lancashire border, high in the Pennines. The church used to send itinerant priests to outlying communities; indeed there was a special Priests' Way linking Dewsbury with Almondbury, Huddersfield, Kirkburton and Kirkheaton. Dewsbury Church was therefore a Minster in mediaeval times and today there are moves to reassume that title.

In the walls around the churchyard are fragments of the mediaeval vicarage and a 13th century doorway. Close by was the Moot Hall, or court — a simple 13th century building with tracery windows. It was demolished in 1963 to make way for road widening.

The church itself dates back to the 12th century but has been substantially altered. The tower was designed by York architect John Carr in 1767. The church was later restored in 1884-85. Inside are to be found an early English column 1310-40, 14th century stained glass and 15th century bosses, as well as an attractive 13th century font. Behind the altar is an impressive oak reredos

Mill landscape beside the River Colne at Milnsbridge

Top: Peak National Park winter landscape
Bottom: View of Castle Hill from Farnley Tyas

depicting Christ and the 12 apostles, flanked by early monarchs and saints, including St Paulinus. One of the brasses on the wall is in memory of Patrick Brontë father of the famous Brontë sisters, Charlotte, Emily and Anne. Patrick Brontë was curate here between 1809-11. He was born on St Patrick's Day at Emdale, County Down, in 1777, and died in Haworth in June 1861. The church is particularly well known for its fascinating early Christian Saxon carvings. The fragments are thought to be the remains of a cross erected in the late ninth century to commemorate St Paulinus's visit to the area. Among them are the remains of a sculpture of the Virgin and Child, the oldest of its kind in Britain. Also on display is a hogback grave covering which, although Danish in inspiration, is one of the earliest known Anglican examples. Another fine coffin lid depicts two entwined dragons. It is carved with attractive animal ornamentation. Along the walls are some 17th century gravestones whose carvings and decoration are very reminiscent of those found on oak furniture of the period.

One of Dewsbury's traditions was commemorated on the 1986 Christmas stamps. The tolling of the Devils's Knoll on Christmas Eve arose when one Thomas de Soothill, a local nobleman and lord of the manor, killed a servant boy in a fit of temper. Sir Thomas hid the boy's body in Forge dam, but was worried about the effect of the murder on his soul and so, as an act of repentance, presented the church with a 13cwt tenor bell with the instructions that, on Christmas Eve, the bell, Black Tom, should be tolled at a slow funeral pace, with one toll for every year since Christ was born, finishing on the stroke of midnight. Inscribed on the bell are the following words: "I shall be here if treated just/when you are mouldering in the dust".

𝕏 *From the church turn left along Wilton Street up to Saville Bridge, over the River Calder.*

From here you can still see many of the woollen, shoddy and mungo mills and dyehouses which created Dewsbury's prosperity. The river originally provided water power for the mills but later was used to provide water for steam power. Around each mill complex there would have been an engine house and chimney, warehouses and workers' terraces.

𝕏 *Retrace your steps back to the Church. Cross the main road and walk straight ahead up Church Street, once known as Priests' Lane, past the Market Inn. At the Market Inn look out for the little carved devil on the far side wall. Follow the road round past Tithe Barn Street and the Wellington Inn.*

The Wellington Inn was at once a centre of revolutionary activity. In 1840, radical agitators seized control of the town and it became the northern centre of the revolutionary movement. Orators harangued the mob from the market cross. Troops were eventually stationed in Dewsbury to maintain order.

🚶 *Carry on and turn right into the Market Place. Go through the Arcade on the left.*

The Arcade was built in 1899 and was Dewsbury's first covered shopping mall. It has recently been restored to reveal its attractive wooden-fronted shop fronts. Turn right and then left to the market.

The wholesale market was established in 1886 and provides space for more than 200 stall-holders. The fine covered market, with its elegant painted iron work and glass canopy, was built in 1904.

🚶 *Turn right into Corporation Street. Turn left and go along Foundry Street, or go through the Market to the large four-storey warehouse ahead, at the top of Whitehall Way.*

This is Cloth Hall Mills, built in 1863 on the site of the old Cloth Hall. It belongs to Machells Brothers, Shoddy and Mungo Merchants. It is this warehouse whose painted sign can be seen from the train on the approach to Dewsbury from Leeds. On the side of the mill can be seen four carved stone faces which are said to be Disraeli, Gladstone and the two Machell brothers.

To the left, looking along Northgate, is the grand Dewsbury Pioneers Cooperative Society building (1878-9) with its elaborate detail and clock tower.

🚶 *Turn right towards the railway viaduct and then turn left along Dewsbury Ring Road, back towards the railway station, passing some particularly fine Italianate warehouses, including that of wool merchant James Howgate.*

Holmfirth – typical Yorkshire weaving town

A walk round Holmfirth

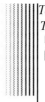

Holmfirth is served by a regular bus service (Yorkshire Rider 309, 310) from Huddersfield Bus Station. Alternatively follow Walk 9 for a more leisurely way of exploring Last of the Summer Wine Country

Holmfirth

SET in a steep wooded valley surrounded by the Pennine hills, Holmfirth is a town of narrow cobbled lanes, secluded courtyards and winding ginnels. The terraces of weavers' cottages with their long rows of mullioned windows and the impressive mills and weaving sheds huddled in the valley bottom reflect the importance of textile production to the town's history.

The town was the victim of three great floods, in 1777, 1852 and 1944. The 1852 flood was caused by the collapse of the dam containing Bilberry Reservoir, which led to the drowning of 81 people. Livestock perished and mills and houses were destroyed when 100 million gallons of water swept through the town. The 1944 flood was caused by a heavy cloudburst in which the River Holme rose by 18ft, flooding nearly 200 houses and killing three people. Today Holmfirth is protected from flooding, but throughout the town are small plaques which record the height of the flood waters.

Compo pops in at Sid's Café

The popular BBC television series, *Last of the Summer Wine*, is filmed in and around Holmfirth, and many of its streets, shops and quiet corners will be familiar from the television screen. This has resulted in Holmfirth becoming a major tourist centre, with many shops and businesses benefiting from the TV boom. On the other hand, there can be congestion at popular times — another reason to use the excellent public transport network (Yorkshire Rider double-decker buses also frequently star in *Last of the Summer Wine* episodes) to avoid adding to traffic congestion and parking problems.

The town trail

🚶 *The walk begins outside the bus station by a tall stone column.*

This column is known locally as "Th' owd Genn". It was erected in 1801 to commemorate the short Peace of Amiens. The Column also has a plaque showing the height of the 1852 flood.

🚶 *Cross the road by the public toilets and take the small cobbled Daisy Lane, opposite, to the rear of the Parish Church.*

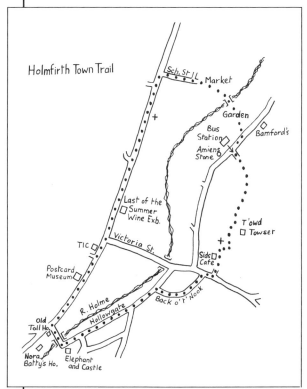

Close to the church is a curiously shaped building, known locally as "Th' owd Towzer", which is thought to be the oldest building in Holmfirth. It dates from 1597 and was originally the church lockup. It has since served a variety of functions which have included a mortuary, ambulance station, gaol and fire station. At the back of "Th' owd Towzer" is a series of interesting ginnels and weavers' cottages, with such evocative names as "Rattle Row". They are well worth exploring.

🚶 *From "Th' owd Towzer" take the right fork, down some steps that lead down to a small paved square and the Parish Church.*

Although there may have been an earlier wooden church on this site, the first stone church was built in 1476 and replaced by a larger building in 1632. The present church is Georgian and was built in 1777-78 in neoclassical style, to the designs of Joseph Jagger, and has an elegant galleried interior. One of the incumbents, a Reverend Edmund Robinson, was accused in 1688 of being a "coiner", clipping coins and then using the metal to manufacture counterfeits. He was convicted and was hanged at York.

Opposite the church is Sid's Café, a former hardware shop which has permanently adopted its *Last of the Summer Wine* television identity — an interesting case of real life having to imitate fiction and a reflection of the power of television.

🚶 *Go up the steps to the left of Sid's Café and continue to the road. Turn right down the hill to the main road. Cross the road and look for a narrow alleyway between two shops straight ahead. This is known as Back o' t' Nook and is said to be the original mediaeval road through Holmfirth. Go through the alleyway past the Nook Pub and cobbler's shop. Turn left along Hollowgate to the Elephant and Castle.*

Hollowgate was once part of the old turnpike road which ran from Enterclough Bridge to Woodhead by way of Holme Moss, and will be familiar to television viewers as a location for *Last of the Summer Wine*. The Elephant and Castle is an 18th century pub which was once a coaching inn on the turnpike road. Another brass plaque near the door indicates the height of floodwater in 1944.

🚶 *At the Elephant and Castle cross the bridge and turn right to the Wrinkled Stocking and Norah Batty's house. Retrace your steps back to the bridge and the Old Toll House book shop, built on the site of the original turnpike toll bar. Turn right along the main road to Bamford's Postcard Museum, above the Library.*

This unusual museum houses a huge collection of saucy seaside postcards published by a local company, Bamford's, which, for more than a century, has produced a huge range of postcards, silent movies, song and hymn sheets and lantern slides. The museum also has a moving audio-visual presentation of the terrible 1852 flood.

🚶 *Continue along the main road past the Tourist Information Centre on the left. Just after the traffic lights is The Last of the Summer Wine Exhibition.*

This exhibition is compulsory for all devotees of the adventures of Compo, Foggy and Clegg. There are photographs and memorabilia from previous series, including the "Utterthwaite personalised self-generating exploratory marine capsule" for rescuing false teeth, old mattresses and supermarket trolleys from the bottom of Kirklees canals!

🚶 *Walk a few yards further down the road and then turn right down School Street to the market.*

Holmfirth market takes place on the left hand side of the car park every Thursdays. Between Easter and Christmas there is a special Saturday craft market selling a range of pottery, woodware, knitwear and other crafts.

⋏ Continue down the hill to the foot bridge. Go over the bridge and straight ahead into the gardens.

Overlooking the gardens is Bamford's, Fine Art, publishers of postcards and greeting cards, with its painted sign and large studio windows. The firm was established in 1870 by an artist, James Bamford, who painted the background for thousands of life models for lantern slides to illustrate songs and stories before the days of cinema. Bamford's was one of the pioneers of motion pictures, well before Hollywood and, between 1908 and 1914, produced films, mainly comedies, using local artists and the general public. The firm ceased making films during World War One and did not resume production. In the meantime Edwin Bamford, son of the founder, had found immediate success in 1902 with the production of postcards from lantern slides depicting popular songs. When interest in these declined around 1918, he introduced comic cards and coloured views which have remained popular to the present day.

Parish Church, Holmfirth

⋏ From the gardens turn right through the main gateway and go back to the bus station. Some buses back to Huddersfield depart from the Council Offices near the traffic lights.

A walk round Huddersfield

Huddersfield

UNTIL the mid-18th century, Huddersfield was a relatively small, inconspicious Pennine town whose local economy was based on weaving and farming and of whose inhabitants John Wesley commented: "A wilder people I never saw in England."

Yet, within 60 years, the town was to expand into a major trading centre, known throughout the world for its fine worsted cloth. It was an expansion stimulated by two important influences — the intervention of the Ramsden family and the coming of the railways.

The Ramsdens were Lords of the Manor who had been granted the estate around Huddersfield in the reign of Elizabeth I. In the 17th century they gained Royal Assent for a market and, in the next two centuries, were responsible for the building of the Cloth Hall, the construction of two canals, turnpike roads, the railways and the redevelopment of the town by Joseph Kaye, a local builder and mason.

Huddersfield Broad Canal near Deighton

Under the direction of Sir William Tite, the eminent Victorian architect employed by the Ramsdens, Huddersfield was provided with a series of wide, grid-patterned streets lined with two storey buildings of locally quarried Crosland Moor stone with main vistas with views towards the surrounding Pennines. Fredrich Engels was to comment in 1844 that Huddersfield was "handsomest by far of all the factory towns of Yorkshire and Lancashire by reason of its charming situation and modern architecture".

The Ramsdens sponsored an Improvement Act in 1820 and the construction of the gas works in 1821 to provide street lighting, but it was the coming of the railway in 1847 that was to be a major stimulus to the town's expansion away from the Market Place to the area around the station. The railway further accelerated the expansion of the textile industry along the Colne Valley trans- forming the factory pattern which has orginally been established by the two Huddersfield Canals. The area around Huddersfield was to lead the West Riding in the introduction of the Jacquard Loom enabling the production of tweeds and woollens for the popular market. Huddersfield produced much of the material used for the traditional cloth caps of the northern working man. Yet it was not only for woollen worsteds that Huddersfield became known, but also for chemical dyes and more recently as the home of Standard Fireworks.

In 1920 Huddersfield Corporation purchased the Ramsden estate including almost all the town centre from the 6th baronet, Sir John Frecheville Ramsden, earning Huddersfield the affectionate title - 'the town that bought itself'.

The town trail

𝕂 *Begins at the Railway Station in St. George's Square.*

Huddersfield Railway Station has one of the finest neo-classical facades of any station in England, 416 feet (129 metres) long and dominating the Square. The station was designed by James Pritchard of York and built by the gifted local builder and mason Joseph Kaye at a cost of £20,000. The foundation stone was laid by Lord Fitzwilliam in 1846 and was marked by a public holiday in the town to celebrate Huddersfield's entrance to the Railway Age. The station opened in 1850 and was designed to symbolise the cooperation between the Lancashire and Yorkshire Railway and the London North Western Railway which operated the two important lines out of Huddersfield. The central portion of the station with its grand projecting portico supported by eight 68 feet high Corinithian columns was originally a hotel and the booking hall of each com- pany was on either side. You can still see the crests of each com- pany above the doorways either side of the main station entrance.

The area in front of the station was left as a public square and is bounded by the George Hotel (1850), The Lion Buildings (1852- 54) and Britannia Buildings. The Lion Chambers were designed as an arcade of shops, storage and offices for the wool merchants. The buildings are decorated with a magnificent lion. The original lion was moved some years ago and the present beast is, in fact, a replica moulded from fibre glass. To the right of the station are the Italinate Britannia buildings with a fine sculpture of Britannia stand- ing above the Royal Arms. Now the Yorkshire Building Society, the

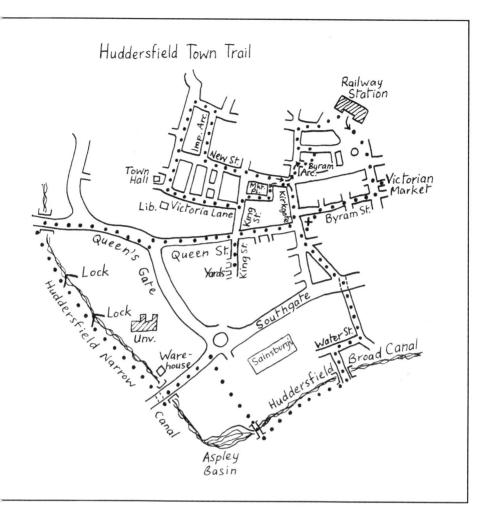

Huddersfield Town Trail

building was originally designed in 1856-9 as warehouses and offices for Huddersfield's expanding wool trade.

🚶 *Walk across the Square towards the Lion Chambers, and cross the main road. Turn left and then right down Northumberland Street. Take the first left to the Victorian Market with its ornate cast iron work and glazed walls.*

The covered market was built between 1887-89 and orginally served as a wholesale market but now has been beautifully restored. It serves as a general market on Monday and Thursday and a bric-a brac market on Tuesday and Saturday.

🚶 *Return to Northumberland Street and cross the road and continue down Bryam Street to the right of the main Post office.*

*Top: Colne Valley
'millscape'
Right: Birch trees
at the edge of
Digley Reservoir*

On the left is the elegant Bulstrode Buildings of 1880. Just before the Parish Church on the left is the old churchyard which has been landscaped to form the attractive St. Peter's Gardens. At the far end of the gardens is the tomb of Joseph Kaye (1780-1858), who was responsible for many of the finest buildings in Huddersfield, including the railway station, Queen Street Chapel and the Royal Infirmary. There are also some interesting 17th century gravestones.

Huddersfield's Parish Church in Kirkgate was built between 1836 and 1838 to the design of J P Pritchett in Gothic style, replacing an earlier church which had fallen into decay exacerbated by lack of finance and a local populace which had become largely nonconformist and therefore unwilling to pay for its upkeep. The church rebuilding was therefore grant aided from the Waterloo Church Fund, established after the defeat of Napoleon to build new churches to help stem the tide of growing nonconformism. The Church has an interesting galleried interior and elaborate altar canopy.

Having left the church continue round the outside down to the main lynch gate.

Close by is the octagonal vestry decorated with carved faces, one of which is of Benjamin Disraeli.

Go through the lynch gate and turn left down Kirkgate past the Boy and Barrel.

If you look up over the doorway you will see the splendid carved figure of the boy sitting astride his barrel.

At the main road (Southgate) turn left to the subway and cross the road. Continue straight ahead via some steps, past the Southgate Nursery. At the road junction turn right into Water Street and then left down Quay Street to the canal bridge.

More reminiscent of a·Dutch waterway than a West Yorkshire canal, Locomotive Bridge was built in 1865 and designed with a system of weights to lift up vertically to allow barges to pass along Huddersfield Broad Canal.

From here are fine views towards the Pennines and across to Castle Hill.

The summit of Castle Hill

This canal was built by Sir John Ramsden to link Huddersfield with the existing canal network to Leeds, Wakefield and the Humber ports enabling the expansion of trade. The canal was authorised by Parliament in 1774 and completed six years later. It runs from the junction of the Calder Hebble Navigation at Cooper Bridge to Kings Mill, Aspley Basin. The canal is $3^1/_2$ miles long and rises 93 feet over 9 locks. It was built under the direction of Luke Holt.

𝕜 *Go over the bridge and turn right along the towpath passing the landscaped frontage of Sainsbury's on the opposite bank. At Ramsden Landing cross Aspley Basin, by the elegant arched bridge over the pool.*

Aspley Basin is the terminus of the Huddersfield Broad Canal and its former junction with the Huddersfield Narrow Canal. For many years it was a focal point of trade and activity with warehouses, mills, offices and accommodation for canal workers. It was here that goods brought along the Huddersfield Narrow Canal were transfered from narrow boats to the larger barges bound for the east coast ports. Two fine 18th century warehouses still stand alonside the canal which are currently being restored as part of the regeneration of the canal basin.

𝕜 *Continue straight ahead past Sainsbury's car park turning left into Wakefield Road over the canal bridge, then take the steps back down to the Huddersfield Narrow Canal towpath under the road.*

The Huddersfield Narrow Canal was authorised by Act of Parliament in 1794 and opened in 1811 to link Huddersfield with the Ashton Canal in Manchester, making it the shortest Trans-Pennine waterway. It was built under the supervison of inexperienced Benjamin Outram using a rather inadequate survey undertaken by Nicholas Brown. The construction of the canal proved an immense task and included the excavation of the three mile Standedge Tunnel through the Pennine watershed. Outram retired in 1801 and the famous engineer Thomas Telford oversaw the remainder of the canal's construction. Although the canal was never a financial success, it acted as a major stimulus to industrial expansion along the Colne Valley in villages such as Marsden, Slaithwaite and Milnsbridge, and contributed to Huddersfield's development as a major centre for the manufacture of woollen cloth.

At the other side of the road tunnel is one of the oldest warehouses in Great Britain (now a private house). This was built around 1776 and still has its hoist intact above the loading bays. Close by is a 19th century crane.

𝕜 *Continue along the canal towpath passing the new University of Huddersfield on the left. Follow the towpath past its current terminus, crossing the access road and continuing along its derelict section past two sets of disused locks and under a road bridge passing the multi-storey Friestrog Mills (1869). At the second bridge and blockage of the canal, go up the metal steps which lead onto Queen Street South.*

Queen Street South is also lined with various mills including Fairfield Mills built in 1855, and Broadbents makers of cotton thread.

ⵊ *Turn right in Queen Street South going up and turning right into Queen's Gate, now part of the Ring Road. Walk Down Queen's Road.*

The building on the right is the old Technical College (1881-4), now part of the University. It was in the present Chemistry Faculty that pioneering chemical dyes were developed in the 19th century by George Jarmaine, establishing Huddersfield's synthetic dyeing industry. Further down is St Paul's Church, now used as a concert hall.

ⵊ *Continue to the pedestrian crossing. Cross the Ring Road to bear left into and along Queen Street.*

Queen Street is lined by a series of town houses built in 1830, in the Georgian-style which are now prestiguous offices of solicitors and insurance companies. Further along Queen Street is the County Court built in 1825, as an oval plaque records, as a Court of Requests. Next to the court is the Queen Street Wesleyan Chapel built by Joseph Kaye. It was completed in 1819 at a cost of £8,000. At the time it was the largest of its kind in the world and sat 1,500 people, demonstrating the rapid growth and confidence of the Nonconformist movement in Kirklees.

ⵊ *Turn right down King Street to Wormalds, Goldthorps and Hammond Yards on the left.* ·

These three yards represent some of the atmosphere of early 19th century Huddersfield when houses and workshops were closely packed together in cramped stone courtyards. Some of the houses have steps which lead to upper storeys and mullioned windows.

ⵊ *Retrace your steps to the junction and turn right to continue along Cross Church Street lined with early 19th century buildings.*

Many of these are now hidden behind modern shop fronts; an exception is Booth and Sons, cutlers, who still have their 19th century shop sign.

ⵊ *At the Parish Church turn left up Kirkgate passing the entrance to the modern Packhorse Centre precinct on the left*

The contrasting colours at Digley Reservoir

This was once the site of the Old Packhorse Inn Yard. On the right are the elegant Kirkgate Buildings decorated with a woman's head entwined by a serpent and which are currently being restored.

🚶 *Turn left into Market Place noting the impressive Lloyds Bank (1912) ahead embellished with neo-classical figures.*

Standing in the Market Place is the Market Cross dating from 1671 and the oldest stucture within Huddersfield town centre. The cross was erected by John Ramsden, the first Baronet, when he was granted his Royal Charter to hold a market on the site.

🚶 *Turn left down Market Walk, past Fillans the jewellers, (who still have their late Victorian shop front complete with curved glass and moulded wood surrounds). Cross King Street and continue straight ahead along Victoria Lane to the Square outside the Library and Art Gallery.*

This building was built in 1934 and on either side of the entrance are two immense seated figures representing the inspiration of literature and art. The Art Gallery has a fine collection of paintings and sculptures by mostly British artists including Lowry, Spencer, Moore, Bacon and Hockney.

𝕏 *Turn right up Ramsden Street past the Town Hall with its Concert Hall .*

The Town Hall and Concert Hall (1876) is one of the most famous in the North of England and together with the renowned Father Willis organ has recently been beautifully restored. The Hall hosts concerts from all over the world and is the home of the Huddersfield Choral Society celebrated throughout the world for its performance of The Messiah and many other choral masterpieces. The choir was described by Sir Charles Halle as the best choir he had ever conducted.

𝕏 *Continue up Ramsden Street.*

Note the red terracotta Prudential Building (1897) on the right, and a fine modern mosaic mural by Harold Blackburn on the left, which commemorates Huddersfield's textile industry before the Industrial Revolution. Turn right along Market Street. Look towards the Sainsbury's supermarket ahead.

Where the Supermarket now stands was the Cloth Hall built in 1766 by John Ramsden as a place where handloom weavers from outlying districts could come to sell their cloth. Before the Cloth Hall was built, it is said that merchants improvised market stalls by draping their material over the walls and tombstones in the church-yard in Kirkgate. As trade expanded, the Cloth Hall was enlarged twice in 1780 and 1848. However, with the development of huge textile mills and warehouses, and the increasing need to avoid industrial piracy with the development of more sophisticated weav-ing designs, use of the Cloth Hall declined until it was closed and finally demolished in 1930. The tower can be seen in the grounds of the Tolson Memorial Museum.

𝕏 *Turn right down and walk through Imperial Arcade (erected between 1873-5 and recently refurbished). The Arcade joins New Street, Huddersfield's main shopping street. Turn left along New Street and walk towards the Market Place.*

On either side of New Street are interesting yards linked by alleyways which are well worth exploring.

𝕏 *Turn left up Westgate and cross the road to enter Byram Arcade.*

Byram Arcade is an elegant arcade built in the 1880s and recently sympathetically restored. It has some interesting shops, specialist boutiques and offices, and a vegetarian restaurant.

𝕏 *Go through the glass doors at the far end of the arcade and turn left to Station Street. Cross Station Street by the pedes-trian crossing and turn left back to Westgate turning right, then first right again along Railway Street.*

On the left are the Tite Buildings (1856) which were built in grand Italinate style as textile warehouses and offices. Opposite are the Ramsden Estate Offices (1871-2) decorated with carved foilage, animals and birds as well as the rear view of a naked man, which, it is said, resulted in the dismissal of the workman responsible. The painted shields represent the marriage line of the Ramsden family.

🚶 *Continue along Railway Street to St. George's Square and the Railway Station.*

 Right: mill complex on Huddersfield Broad Canal

Country walks from the Huddersfield Line

Shoddy and Mungo country

Dewsbury to Batley

The lower Calder Valley is full of unexpected delights, despite being in the industrial heartland of Kirklees. This walk provides some exceptional views across a densely packed valley of Victorian mills and chimneys, terraced houses and railway viaducts, while giving the opportunity to discover some fine countryside around Caulms Wood and the villages of Hanging Heaton and Soothill. This way uses part of the Kirklees Way Walk.

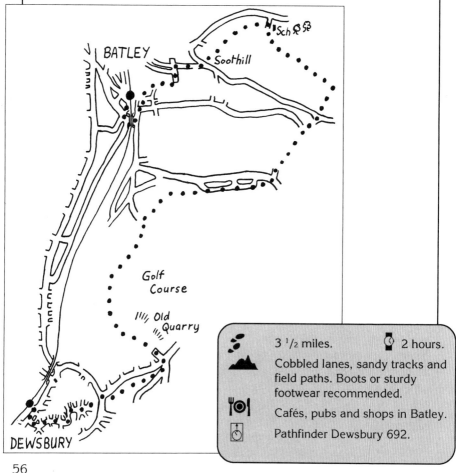

BATLEY

Sch

Soothill

Golf
Course

Old
Quarry

DEWSBURY

3 ¹/₂ miles.   🕐 2 hours.

Cobbled lanes, sandy tracks and field paths. Boots or sturdy footwear recommended.

Cafés, pubs and shops in Batley.

Pathfinder Dewsbury 692.

🚶 From Dewsbury Station cross the road by the pedestrian crossing to Wellington Road and follow the signs to the Magistrates' court. Continue along an attractive cobbled alleyway, passing a fine old warehouse on the left. Go down the steps to the road (Grove Road). Turn right and then left at the road junction, into Daisy Hill. Continue down Daisy Hill and, at the bottom, turn left into the Market Place and head towards the Town Hall. For a description and history of Dewsbury see 'A Walk Round Dewsbury'.

At the Town Hall, go up Old Wakefield Road which runs along the left hand side of the Town Hall. At the car park go up the steps towards the busy main Ring Road. Cross the road with care by the traffic lights, opposite

Weavers' cottages at Honley

the Victorian Baptist church. Continue straight ahead up Leeds Road. Opposite Eastborough Primary School take the cobbled road on the right. Follow the lane past Highbury Terrace, climbing steadily.

🌿 *From here there are some superb panoramic views of Dewsbury.*

At the road junction, turn left and continue along the lane which soon becomes a grassy track. At the road, turn left down to the main road. Cross the road and on the right hand side of The Crown pub is the entrance to Caulms Wood. You can pick up the blue signs for the Kirklees Way at this point.

ℹ️ *Originally used for quarrying and drift mining, Caulms Wood was transformed into the site of the Kirklees Garden Festival and was extensively landscaped with feature gardens, sculptures and children's play areas.*

🌿 *At the entrance is a pyramid sculpture, from where a sandy track gradually ascends the edge of the festival site, providing some superb views of Dewsbury and the Calder valley.*

Follow this sandy track until it begins to descend to the main track below. Take the path on the right through some broom bushes and continue straight ahead through a field following a wall to a stile. Over the stile, continue straight ahead along a clear path (SE 251 229). Ignore the path on the left, and continue to an old stone gap stile and wire fence ahead.

❧ *From here there are magnificent views down to Batley and the main Dewsbury-Leeds railway line.*

Follow the path to a wooden stile and fence just above a row of cottages. Cross the stile and veer right up the hill to some houses and a track. Go left along the track to a road, emerging just below the Fox and Hounds pub. Turn left to the road junction and then right through Hanging Heaton to the church. At this point the Kirklees Way turns left.

ℹ️ Hanging Heaton is known locally as Tewitland, a name which is said to derive from the large number or tewits, or peewits, which used to nest in the area. Originally a weaving settlement, there are still many examples of weaving cottages in the village, some of which still retain traces of upper room doorways. Of particular interest is a collection of old houses, ginnels, yards and alleyways near the church, known as "The Folds". The church was built in 1825 and is a "Waterloo church", having been built from the funds made available by the Government to celebrate the victory over Napoleon. The outside is decorated with a series of grotesque heads and faces.

Go through the lychgate, past the church and the Georgian vicarage, to the road. Take the signed footpath opposite, along an enclosed path leading to a field. At the field, veer right to cross a muddy lane and keep straight ahead, towards Grange Farm. At the farm, continue along the lane, climbing gently to a "crossroads" of paths (SE 264 238). Turn left along a waymarked field path alongside the fence to a stile.

❧ *From here there are magnificent views across the Greenhill valley towards Hanging Heaton Church, and down to the huge mill complexes around Batley.*

Continue past the school and then turn sharp left (SE 258 243) down a signed footpath to a stile in the corner. Over the stile continue down the hill, keeping the hedge on your left. Go over the second stile to the lane and walk down to the road. At the road turn right into Soothill and walk towards Soothill Hall on your left.

ℹ️ The name Soothill derives from the de Soothill family who, in mediaeval times, were Lords of the Manor. The present Hall dates from the early 1800s, although part of the structure dates back to the 16th century.

Walk past Soothill Hall and take the footpath on the left, over the old railway bridge. Veer right between wire fences past the premises of the Lay-E-Zee bedding company, which is the largest in Europe, producing 3,500 complete mattresses and divans a week. At the road, turn right and follow the road under the railway viaduct. Turn right up Back Station Road and then take the narrow cobbled alleyway on the right, which leads directly up to the forecourt of Batley Station.

Hopton Woods and Briestfield

Ravensthorpe to Mirfield

This is a walk of great beauty and contrast in east Kirklees, taking advantage of paths through Hopton Woods, and crossing little known, and surprisingly rural valleys close to the centres of both Mirfield and Dewsbury.

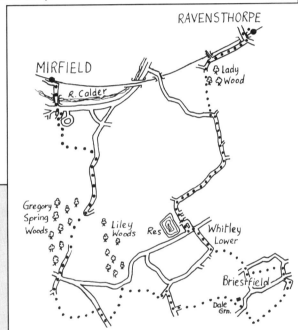

7 miles.

4 hours.

Field paths and tracks; some careful pathfinding required, and some muddy stretches after rain, especially along the well used bridleways. Boots recommended.

Pubs at Whitley Lower, Briestfield and Houses Hill; cafés, shops, pubs in Mirfield.

Pathfinder Sheet 703 Wakefield South. Walk this way route – Hopton Wood Circular

Breakpoint:

Briestfield (three miles) Yorkshire Woollen District Bus 200 back to Dewsbury (Sundays 210 from Whitley Lower only).

ᛣ   From the exit drive at Ravensthorpe Station, pass the old mill
and turn left in the lane, crossing back over the railway line. Take
the first track on the right, with a "Walk this Way" sign, and go
alongside the railway following the red waymarks. Follow the track
down to a junction by the bridge over the railway where you turn
left through the woods, avoiding a boggy section of track to reach a
broad stone causeway climbing into Lady Wood. Continue to where
the track bends right to meet a route coming in from your left at a
junction. Turn left here, and follow this path as it in turn goes to the
right at a second junction, past woods (Jordan Woods) and a golf
course. For much of the way it is a lovely paved causeway enclosed
by woods and hedgerows. Tree species to be seen in this hedge
include hawthorn, hazel, blackthorn and field maple.

As you reach the top of the hill the path joins a farm track. Keep
ahead to a broader junction where you turn left past the reservoir
into Whitley Lower, where you'll find a post office and the Woolpack
Inn.

Turn left, but take the first lane on the right, a cul-de-sac,
Howroyd Lane, soon passing the early Victorian church of St Mary
and Michael. Keep ahead to where the lane bends right past a white
cottage, where a metal stile in the corner leads to a path down
narrow, concrete steps. This is a particularly beautiful path, descending through arching oak, elder and hawthorn trees by old
mine workings. Continue down to a footbridge over Howroyd Beck
then over stiles and up the side of the hedge ahead to a lane along
the top of the ridge.

Cross and take the lane which goes almost directly ahead in the
same direction, but after 80 metres go through the stile on the left,
signed, which leads to a field path. Keep straight ahead, parallel
with the lane, past the remains of a gap stile by a wall and into the
next field, then over a stone step stile ahead, keeping immediately
to the right of the farm ahead where a gate leads to the access road
to the lane by Briestfield.

Turn right in Briestfield, down to the Shoulder of Mutton inn on
the lane corner. From here take the lane on the right, which slopes
steeply downhill, but in the corner at the bottom of the hill where
the lane bears right, keep ahead along a track over Briestfield Beck
which ascends to a field gate. This gives access to a stony lane
between field walls. Turn right into the lane, with fine views towards
Yorkshire Television's Emley Moor transmitter on your left as you
ascend.

Keep going straight ahead past a farm, Healey, and a junction
with a track on the left, about 50 metres beyond which there is a
wooden stile in the fence on the right. Go over this, and walk
straight across and down the field over the dip in the hillside to
where you'll see a stile leading to a footbridge over the beck. The

Mediaeval tower at Mirfield

path ascends to another stile then bears slightly right over rough land to a stone stile in the lane ahead (SE 227 170).

Cross, continuing directly ahead, over another stile by the edge of a gentrified farmhouse, Dale Green. Keep ahead along the side of the next field, to two stiles crossing a green track (a private way). This second stile leads into a large arable field which the path crosses diagonally to a stone gap stile a few metres to the right of the opposite corner, though you may prefer to go round the edge of the field to avoid a crop. The path now goes across the field more or less parallel with the pylons on the right, before veering to the right and dropping to the farm, Clock Royd, on the right. Go through the gate into the farmyard and left along the farm track into the lane below Falhouse Green (SE 219 170).

Once in the lane turn right, ignoring the first footpath sign almost directly ahead, but going down the hill for some 100 metres before taking a signed path along a farm track on the left. Keep going straight ahead, past the farm and its large round slurry tank, heading on tractor tracks uphill to the gateway, behind which is a free-standing metal footpath sign. Turn right here, going along the hedge and fence to the field corner, before turning left alongside the fence under pylons. This path reaches a step stile into a narrow enclosed path which contours around a curve in the hillside above Lilley Woods (SE 214 172). Turn left here and follow the path to the main road (B6118). Turn right for 90 metres to where a step stile on the left leads to a field path passing what appears to be a classical temple on the brow of the hill to the right.

ℹ️ This monument, known locally as The Temple, or Black Dick's Tower, was the summer house of Whitley Hall, demolished many years ago. The hall was reputed to be haunted by one Sir Richard Beaumont, a 17th century owner of Whitley Hall who, either because of his swarthy appearance or his wicked deeds, was known as "Black Dick of the North" by King James I.

There is no access to Black Dick's Tower. Bear slightly left to a stile in the fence along the ridge.

☆ There is a glorious viewpoint across to Fenay Bridge and Kirkburton, with the high Pennines beyond.

Go ahead and slightly left to a stile through a narrow strip of wood by a track. Cross the wood. The path now heads half left towards a huge farm complex below; keep outside the enclosed area to join the overgrown drive leading to the main gate. Turn right along this drive until it meets a farm track from Gregory Farm at a stile (SE 205 171), following it uphill to the main road.

Directly opposite by Moxon's depot and Lilley Hall Farm is a track, through gates, which leads gently downhill past Gregory Spring Woods.

❀ Superb views on all sides.

🅸 Gregory Spring Woods, like most of Hopton Woods, are ancient, semi-natural woodlands which have remained relatively undisturbed for centuries. Beech is now dominant, and this is a favourite place for wild flowers in the spring, as well as being good for birdlife.

Follow this stony track down through the woods for a little less than half a mile to a junction beyond a gate — your way is to the left, dipping down across a shallow valley before ascending into an enclosed path. Just before you reach a farmhouse (Boyd's Farm), on the right, look for a wooden stile on the left which leads to a narrow path across the fields. Take this, crossing stiles across another track, then dipping down by hedgerows and bridging a beck before bearing right alongside Briery Bank Woods on the outskirts of Mirfield. Keep straight ahead, as the path becomes a narrow enclosed way, past backs of houses and gardens (look for waymarks as the path zigzags between houses), finally turning right and emerging by squeezer stiles in Granny Lane, at the road junction by the Flower Inn. Turn right across the River Calder and pass allotments to the railway bridge and Mirfield Station — the nearside platform for Huddersfield and Manchester, far side for Dewsbury, Wakefield and Leeds. The centre of Mirfield lies along Station Road ahead, towards the main Huddersfield Road.

Top: Royal Farm near Meltham Right: The old wharf at Mirfield on the Calder-Hebble Navigation

The Mirfield Ginnels

Mirfield Circular

Ginnels are typical features of the old West Riding — narrow enclosed alleyways which form pedestrian through routes in built-up areas. This short but unusual urban stroll from Mirfield Station to the town's Victorian church and adjacent mediaeval tower makes use of a section of towpath along the historic Calder-Hebble Navigation, a park — and some attractive interlinking ginnels.

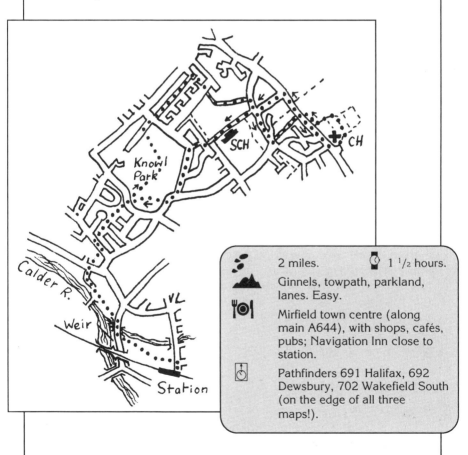

2 miles.　　🕐 1 ½ hours.

Ginnels, towpath, parkland, lanes. Easy.

Mirfield town centre (along main A644), with shops, cafés, pubs; Navigation Inn close to station.

Pathfinders 691 Halifax, 692 Dewsbury, 702 Wakefield South (on the edge of all three maps!).

人　From Mirfield Station exit walk up Station Road towards the town centre but about 100 metres beyond the railway bridge, turn left along a track which leads past the Navigation Inn and behind Mirfield Canal Basin and Boatyard, along a narrow enclosed path between high fences and walls. This emerges in Newgate Road; turn right but, immediately over the bridge, follow the cobbled path onto the towpath of the Calder-Hebble Navigation, past grassy wharfs and benches, with fine views across to the weir where the main River Calder rejoins the Navigation beyond Mirfield locks.

ℹ *The Calder-Hebble Navigation, one of Yorkshire's oldest working waterways, dates from 1758, when powers were granted to make the River Calder navigable between Wakefield and Sowerby Bridge, including canal sections or "cuts", such as this one, to avoid the need for weirs. It was opened in 1770 and, by 1804, linked at Sowerby Bridge with the Rochdale Canal to form an important trans-Pennine waterway.*

Follow the path as it swings right and past a group of cottages to emerge on the main Huddersfield Road. The first ginnel (signed) lies almost directly opposite, cutting between houses onto Nettleton Road. Turn left for a short distance and then first right down another fairly modern alleyway by gardens; where this bends right, take the fork left past bungalows, keeping right at the top to reach Knowl Road, opposite Knowl Park.

Cross into the park and ascend towards the playing field at its far end before turning left and heading for a path in the left hand corner by the hedge, which leads into Beechwood Avenue, a modern estate road. Follow this up to its junction with Beechwood Road and turn right. Almost immediately opposite is another fascinating ginnel which leads behind gardens parallel to West Royd Avenue. Where this ends, turn right into yet another ginnel behind more gardens and a large school playing field. This turns sharp left past the edge of the playing field and leads into Sousa Lane; bear right here into Towngate. Follow Towngate to where it bends to the right, continuing straight ahead into Pinfold Lane, but look for a ginnel on the left which leads alongside the old railway line and up to Dunbottle Lane. Turn right along here to Mirfield Church.

ℹ *Mirfield's striking hilltop church was designed by the great Victorian architect, Sir Giles Gilbert Scott, in 1871; equally interesting is the tower of the early 13th century church which stands behind the newer building. The top part of the tower was added in Victorian times. Immediately to the west of the present church lie the foundations of a mediaeval motte and bailey castle.*

Follow the path which leads round the outside of the church and graveyard; at the junction of paths bear left alongside the wall to join another ginnel by the old railway; go left here back to Dunbottle Lane. Turn right over the old railway bridge, keeping ahead to the junction with Camm Lane and turning left past some attractive old cottages. This emerges back at the school playing field by Sousa Lane.

The next ginnel leads almost directly ahead between the Secondary School and the playing field, past the school buildings, then across Westfields Avenue into Westfield Road.

Turn left downhill, once again passing Knowl Park. Look for an opening into the park on the right hand corner; cross the parkland and head for the bus stop on Knowl Road, just beyond which is the start of the ginnel leading back to Nettleton Road and Huddersfield Road. Retrace your steps along the Navigation towpath and back to Mirfield Station.

Along Huddersfield's canals to Golcar

Deighton to Slaithwaite

Mills dominate this walk which follows Sir John Ramsden's Broad Canal through the centre of Huddersfield, before following the towpath of the Huddersfield New Canal into the Colne Valley, and climbing to the remarkable hand-loom weaving hillside settlement of Golcar.

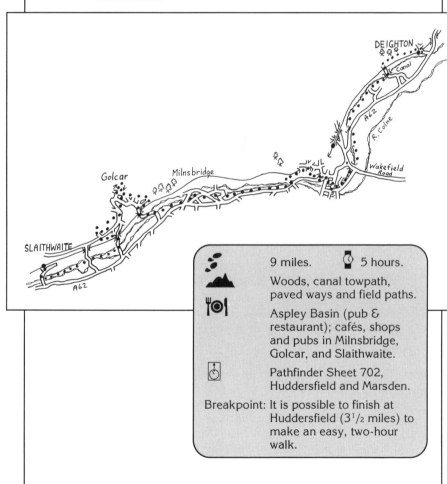

9 miles.   5 hours.

Woods, canal towpath, paved ways and field paths.

Aspley Basin (pub & restaurant); cafés, shops and pubs in Milnsbridge, Golcar, and Slaithwaite.

Pathfinder Sheet 702, Huddersfield and Marsden.

Breakpoint: It is possible to finish at Huddersfield (3½ miles) to make an easy, two-hour walk.

🛉   From the exit from Deighton Station turn left into Whitaker Street, continuing for about 120 metres to where, on the left just before the stone bridge over the disused railway line, a path immediately alongside a bungalow slopes to the old railway trackbed.

This informal footpath runs through a deep, grassy cutting before emerging alongside the existing main line railway, with long views across the industrial lower Colne Valley, with Castle Hill in the distance. Continue below Deighton Woods or The Riding, a steep wooded hillside filled with oak, beech and sycamore. Where the path reaches fencing, by a tunnel, bear slightly right to follow a lovely path through the edge of the woods, still parallel to the railway, across a dip eventually to reach a crossing track (SE 156 188). Turn left here, crossing bridges over both the old trackbed and the existing railway, continuing down a cobbled lane past a scrapyard and playing fields and bridge across the Sir John Ramsden Canal, at Fieldhouse Bridge and Locks. Turn right onto and along the canal towpath.

📕 *Sir John Ramsden's Canal was built in 1784 to link the growing town of Huddersfield with the Calder-Hebble Navigation. Three and a half miles long, it cost £11,974 to build, which was recouped with tolls of 1s 6d (7 $^1/_2$p) per ton load. It was also known as the Huddersfield Broad Canal (with locks 14ft wide) to distinguish it from the newer Huddersfield Narrow Canal (7ft wide) which linked with it at Aspley Basin. It is still in operation, at least for leisure*

The Huddersfield Broad Canal near Bradley Mills

traffic, and it provides an extremely attractive green corridor and walkway into the centre of Huddersfield, with some fine bridges, locks and canalside buildings, including mills and warehouses, illustrating the impact the waterway had on the industrialisation of Huddersfield.

Follow the canal for the next two miles past the mills and factories. The tall, light-coloured chimney on the right belongs to the Huddersfield Waste Incinerator. Soon past this, the canal runs alongside, then beneath, the main A62 Leeds Road before passing a handsome Dutch-stile drawbridge, and Sainsburys store, to Aspley Canal Basin (SE 150 165).

▮ Aspley Basin contains a number of impressive 18th and 19th century warehouses and mills, including one of Britain's oldest surviving canal warehouses, complemented by attractive new developments such as the new Sainsburys, with its canalside promenade, and Ramsden's Landing, a themed pub and restaurant.

Cross by the new arched footbridge into the car park, turning left at the main entrance into Wakefield Road, where, just beyond the canal bridge, steps lead back onto the Narrow canal towpath to a tunnel under the road, and alongside the start of the Huddersfield New Canal, through part of Huddersfield University Campus. Where the navigable section of canal ends at a barrier, cross the street to continue along the towpath by the derelict canal, through a canyon of high mill buildings. This ends at the bridge at Queen's Road South where an office block has been built on the route of the canal.

Exit by the steps, crossing and turning right up Queen's Road before turning first left along Milford Street. At the end, cross into Chapel Hill by the Rat and Ratchet pub, turning right up to the Ring Road. Should you decide to end the walk here, keep straight ahead across the Ring Road to Huddersfield town centre and railway station.

Otherwise, cross at the lights and turn left down Manchester Road, past a tall, slightly neglected, early Victorian terrace of pub, nightclub, tattooist and aquarium. Steps at the end of the terrace lead up to Outcote Bank. Cross and turn right here for no more than 50 metres to where a grassy path, looking more like wasteland, goes between the end of an office building and parking area and the wall — this is in fact a public path (SE 142 163). Follow it up past new offices and fenced parking areas till it leads into an estate road of new maisonettes.

Bear right through a traffic-calmed cul-de-sac to a path between houses, towards what looks like the roof of a chapel ahead, but is in fact a handsome Victorian primary school in Water Street. Walk past the school to the end of the street, turning left into Springwood Avenue then first left again into Bow Street where, after 20 metres, a sign on the wall on the right indicates "Springwood Footpath Leading to Paddock". Take this track towards a scrapyard where you'll see a paved, enclosed footpath branching off left — the Springfield Footpath. This passes woods before crossing the Manchester and Sheffield railway lines at a narrow footbridge, with fine views along the Paddock Viaduct and across the Colne Valley, and descending towards Paddock.

Turn left into Gledhow Bank, and left again into Market Street, going under the Crosland Viaduct to the junction with Manchester Road at the traffic lights. Cross here, turning right into Manchester

Road and across the canal bridge past shops, and through the yard of Charlie Brown's garage on the right. An entrance through the wall leads onto the towpath of the restored sections of the Huddersfield Narrow Canal. Turn left, following the canal back under the stone arches

Waterside esplanade at Aspley Basin (note the suspension bridge in the background)

and railway viaduct, soon crossing the River Colne by an aqueduct.

Easy walking follows along the canal towpath which takes a route just above the valley floor, linking mills and workshop areas, passing old cottages and restored locks, but also areas of green countryside. Before Ephraim Woods works, the canal is again blocked by an access road but it continues immediately beyond it, now going past Britannia Mills, a massive complex built in 1861.

Keep going until you reach the outskirts of Milnsbridge, passing more mills, some still in operation, others sadly deserted. The main bridge, carrying Market Street over the canal by the locks, gives access into the centre of this typical Pennine mill town, birthplace of former Prime Minister, Sir Harold Wilson, and offering a choice of shops, cafés and pubs.

Canal and towpath continue around the outskirts of Milnsbridge, before curving over another narrow aqueduct across the River Colne by waterfalls, again passing a fine mill complex. Soon after more locks and a high concrete overbridge from the mill, take the narrow stone bridge on the right (SE 101 156) which leads to a narrow track past newly restored weavers' cottages, and up to Britannia Lane.

Cross and turn right in Britannia Road and walk parallel with the railway for about 300 metres to where, just before the houses on the left, steps lead to a footbridge over the railway. Follow the narrow, Tarmac path uphill past Scar Wood. Where the path bears right up steps, take the narrower path, forking left up well spaced steps to pass more cottages at Kiln Brow. Cross Scarhouse Lane into James Street, but look for the steps on the right just past Jode Cottage, No 26. This emerges behind Knowle Bank School. Turn left into a narrow lane, Handel Street, lined with delightful period cottages, which gradually descends to a junction of ways. Take the level route, ahead but slightly to the left, Clay Well, past a tall, weaver's cottage into Small Lane, but look for a narrow enclosed Tarmac way on the right, up steps, which emerges in Cliffe Ash, almost opposite the Colne Valley Museum and the centre of Golcar.

i *Golcar is one the finest weaving hilltop settlements in York-shire, reflecting the expansion of hand loom weaving between the 17th and early 19th centuries, before the growth of canal-served, steam-powered mills in the valley destroyed their market.*

Rows of hillside cottages that make up the town capture not only glorious views, but excellent southern light for weaving lofts. The Colne Valley Museum, open weekend afternoons 2-5pm, has demonstrations of handloom weaving and clog-making, together with much material illustrating the history of the Colne Valley. There's an example of a Wuzzle Stone (see page 12) to be seen at the back of the museum. Golcar has a town square (with toilets), a Regency Church with a tall spire which makes a striking landmark, a café, shops and two pubs.

Return from the Colne Valley Museum down the enclosed way, turning left into Small Lane, but immediately past Millbank, a tall, stone house with a built-in wide arched coach stable, take the narrow path right, down steps between walls. This goes by the edge of fields to emerge in Brook Lane, by a farmhouse. Cross, and just behind the bus stop, steps descend to a footbridge over a beck behind another mill. Keep ahead up a fieldside, bearing right along a hedge, keeping to its left behind gardens to emerge at Upper Wellhouse (SE 096 153). Cross the road to the lane ahead, go past the junction with Copley Bank Road, along a track into the group of cottages and farms ahead. The track bears right round the outside of a house and garden towards a farm ahead. On the left behind the house (SE 095 152) is a rickety wooden stile. Cross the path, bearing right after 30 metres below and alongside a retaining wall to a stone stile. Keep going across the field to the next stile which is in the centre of the wall ahead; cross to the next stile whose entrance is guarded by a huge stone roller serving as a post. From here the path veers right through an old gap stile in the ruined wall on the right; head for the long, narrow farm buildings at the top end of the field on the right (SE 091 149). A gate leads into a sunken packhorseway, Watroyd Lane. Turn left and walk down to the road.

Almost immediately opposite is a stile which leads to a path descending alongside the remains of a wall, down a large open field, before bearing left through heather to the railway line, follow-ing the line to steps leading through a tunnel, before bearing left to steps into Low Westwood Lane. Turn right for 100 metres to reach the crossing with the canal and towpath. Real ale fanatics might wish to continue along the lane for another 250 metres to where steps on the left lead into Manchester Road at Linthwaite; 300 metres up Hoyle Ing, directly opposite, is the Sair Inn whose home brewed Linfit ales, with such exotic names as Leadboiler, Old Ely and Enoch's Hammer, have a reputation which extends well beyond the boundaries of Kirklees.

But the return to Slaithwaite is in fact directly along the towpath of what is a beautiful stretch of canal, past more mills, a fine mill pond, and a green stretch of valley. Where the canal once again terminates, a Tarmac walkway directly ahead, across lawns between mill buildings, leads through what used to be the old canal basin. There's a café, shops and three pubs, and a manor house (now the Dartmouth Estate Office) with a sundial whose supporting pillar is reputedly a Roman milestone.

Bear right at the fork or cross roads to complete the final few yards uphill to Slaithwaite Station — Huddersfield platforms are immediately beyond the bridge.

Should you decide to extend the walk a further three miles to Marsden Station, the towpath continues directly ahead along the path, through a small area of parkland, past Slaithwaite's old Manor House, where, past a mill, the canal begins again. The walk along the valley, past river, mills and reservoirs is exceptionally beautiful.

Scammonden

Slaithwaite to Marsden

A high level walk from the Colne Valley to explore one of the most dramatic civil engineering features of the Pennines — Scammonden Dam and Reservoir — with glorious views in clear weather.

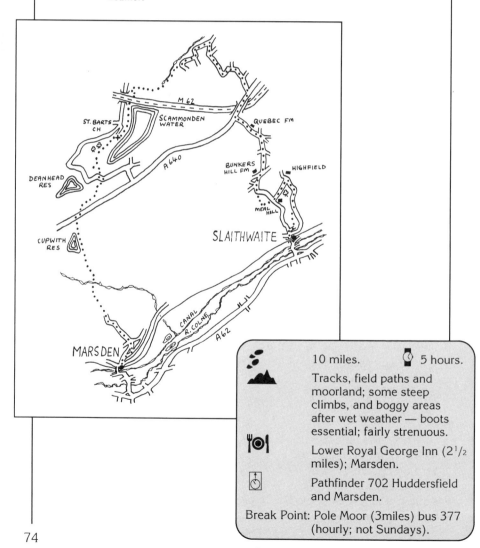

	10 miles.	🕐 5 hours.
	Tracks, field paths and moorland; some steep climbs, and boggy areas after wet weather — boots essential; fairly strenuous.	
🍽	Lower Royal George Inn (2¹/₂ miles); Marsden.	
🕐	Pathfinder 702 Huddersfield and Marsden.	

Break Point: Pole Moor (3miles) bus 377 (hourly; not Sundays).

🚶 If you alight at Slaithwaite Station off the train from Leeds or Huddersfield, follow the station drive to the road, Crimble Bank, turning left under the railway bridge. Immediately beyond the bridge (opposite the entrance to the eastbound platform), turn sharp left up a steep flight of stone steps which zigzag up the hillside. There are soon fine views across the Colne Valley.

Wessenden Valley winter scene

At the top of the steps keep straight ahead across Royd Street, past the corner newsagent's, but take the first road right, Colne Street. About 50 metres on the left, immediately past a stone cottage dated 1685 and called Hill Top Fold, a cobbled track leads into a narrow entry past the top of a series of terraced streets to a Tarmacked road which terminates beyond a bungalow in a cul-de-sac. On the right, immediately past allotment buildings, a grassy path dips into a narrow side valley, Crimble Clough. Below is a huge mill building, and you may well see a Trans-Pennine train speeding over the railway viaduct crossing the valley below.

Follow the path as it descends past gardens and cottages to join a metalled lane. Turn left here, following the lane as its climbs past stone houses up the valley. It gradually narrows, past Crimble Cottage, another 17th century house; beyond Swan Farm it becomes a slightly overgrown footpath climbing a wooded gorge, lined with beech and sycamore.

You emerge at Highfield, a small hamlet of gentrified farms (SE 079 153). Turn left along the main, Tarmacked drive, which becomes Surat Road.

🌿 *Panoramic views along the whole length of the Colne Valley.*

Where the lane meets Meal Hill Lane past a farmhouse, cross to go through the metal field gate ahead, taking the unmarked public path alongside the wall by the edge of the field. In the corner is a wooden hurdle stile; cross, and descend overgrown steps, to a little sunken beck, then climb the bank onto a field path. Turn right, following this grassy path alongside the beck and overgrown holly hedges up a long field, with the masts of Pole Moor wireless transmitter ahead. At Pole Moor, evidence has been found of a Bronze Age cemetery, but as of yet no settlement has been identified. At a gate this enters a track which bears right back to the lane.

Turn left uphill, but at the next bend another sunken green lane on the right leads up to a point below Bunkers Hill farm (SE 074153). Join the track, but immediately past a farm cottage, take the long track, left, which climbs Moorside Edge to the lane ahead by the old quarry. Turn left here, and walk along the lane, past Quebec Farm to its junction with New Hey Road, the A640.

i *The Lower Royal George Inn (SE 069 163) stands immediately on the left. Note the old carved guide stoop or milestone just before the Royal George, with mileages to "Marsden, Huddersfield, Halifax, Marsden Scammanden and Daynhead". It was erected by John Woodhead, Surveyor, in 1755. This post once stood at an important crossroads of packhorse ways and roads nearby, some of them surviving, others altered by the motorway. The present A640 follows the line of what, in turn, was (probably) a prehistoric ridgeway, a Roman Road and an early 19th century turnpike. The Royal George, originally a packhorse inn, stood at the boundary of several ancient townships — the guide post still marks the boundary between Kirklees and Calderdale.*

To continue, turn right and follow the main road (with a good sidewalk) across the M62 motorway, keeping straight ahead for another quarter of a mile to its junction with Marsden Gate. Go left here, but at the first bend, where there is a house, follow the footpath sign by taking the track below and to the left of the house. Follow the track, which contours to the right above a shallow gulley. At the junction of tracks, take the path left, down to Dean House Lane, which drops steeply down past Lower Moulson Place before swinging right along the valley, past Dean Cottages.

At the next signed junction, take the path signed to Firth House Mill, down the grassy track to the ruined farmhouse of Dean House (SE 063174) on an elevated position above the valley. Just before the farm, a stone step stile on the right leads to a grassy track downhill. Look down the valley to the mill chimney on the left, with twin stone houses on the right, separated by a large field. A narrow gap stile in a ruined wall leads to a path alongside the wall to steps in the lane below.

Turn left and follow the narrow lane across Red Lane Dike, into and through the mill complex, now housing Jordan Engineering works. The lane climbs past the chimney and twists right uphill away from the stream. But, where it forks, take the right fork, with the Calderdale Countryside signs, for Scammonden. Past the farm, (SE 058 174) a wooden stile on the right, waymarked, leads to a path alongside a fence above a shallow valley. Follow the path ahead, over more stiles, to a wood, where you head alongside the gaunt remains of a ruined mill. Keep in the same direction over fallen stones, before bearing right down to the stream, Black Brook, near Scammonden Dam pumping station, where a footbridge takes the path a short distance uphill to a stile. Head up the hillside and slightly to the right to the ruined farm ahead, Lower Hey House (SE 052 172). From here a sunken green lane ascends the hillside, bearing left, then sharp right, to join the Tarmacked lane above. Turn left.

There are magnificent views of the Scammonden Dam from here. This 242ft high, 1,050ft long dam, which required five million cubic yards of material in its construction, was opened by the Queen in 1971. A unique feature is the fact that it was designed to combine a six-lane highway — the superbly engineered M62 trans-Pennine motorway — with its function as a reservoir dam. The reservoir itself — Scammonden Water — covers 104 acres when full, is 170ft deep at its deepest point and is almost a mile long. It holds 1.7 million gallons of water.

The lane soon terminates at a Yorkshire Water Company gate on the left. Access is by a stile on the left of the gate. Descend the track to the gated entrance on the right to the tunnel under the motorway, which leads directly into Scammonden Countryside Park.

This is an area of woodland, open grassland, informal foot-paths, and picnic areas around Scammonden Water. More than 30 species of birds are regularly recorded, along with a rich botanic life. Once away from the roar of motorway traffic, the lake, with its magnificent moorland setting and colourful dinghies of the Scammonden Sailing Club, is remarkably peaceful.

Keep walking directly ahead onto a narrow, marked path which passes birch and larch woods and descends to the water's edge, before meandering uphill and reaching a crossing point below Deanhead Church. Turn right up steps to Deanhead Church. Turn left to the gate into the churchyard.

St Bartholomew's Church, with its little bell tower, was built in 1863 to replace two earlier structures. The church, with its quite extensive graveyard, remains very much in use, serving a scattered moorland community. The old National School of 1824 is now the village school.

Leave the churchyard through the gate, turning left to a gate and stile at the end of the track. This leads to a lovely elevated path, Brooke Walk; at a fork, keep left down to the head of the reservoir, but at the second crossing of paths at a wooden signpost (SE 043 156) descend to a wooden footbridge, turning right alongside the stream to a stile into the picnic area and car park. A second stile almost immediately on the left leads to a path which crosses to the wood ahead — turn right by the wooden sign alongside the stream, crossing the stream along a sunken way to the lane at a layby.

Go left here, uphill, but after 100 metres look for an elaborate stone step stile on the right (SE 044 153). A path bears right up a shallow gulley from here, becoming a deep, very overgrown track. Pick your way up it, to where it levels and go through a gate and stile into a sunken green lane. There are fine views of Deanhead Reservoir, built as long ago as 1840, to the right. Keep ahead to the stile leading into Watermans Farm, with its amazing collection of vehicles and timber. Then follow the farm track to the main road.

Go right for 100 metres, then over the stile on the left, waymarked "Kirklees Way", leading to a cindery track past Cupwith Reservoir. Keep ahead, past a stone memorial seat (SE 040 138), over Slaithwaite Moor, fording a small stream (look out for boggy patches) to Netherwood Heys Hill, from where the path follows the wallside before entering a green lane, Huck Hill Lane.

❧ There are superb views across and down into the Colne Valley from here, with Marsden and its mills set against a background of green hills. There are views to and beyond the reservoirs of the Wessenden Valley, into the hills of the Peak National Park.

At a crossing of tracks, follow the "Colne Valley Walk" waymark, through a pedestrian gate by the side of the farm ahead, leading down a green way; take the left fork which descends to another track by cottages. Turn right here to emerge in Marsden by the station bridge, with the welcoming Railway Inn close by.

Rapes Highway and Standedge

Marsden circular

This is one of the most spectacular walks in the South Pennines, taking in a number of historic features of transport interest — an ancient packhorse way, early turnpike roads, a canal and the Pennine Way.

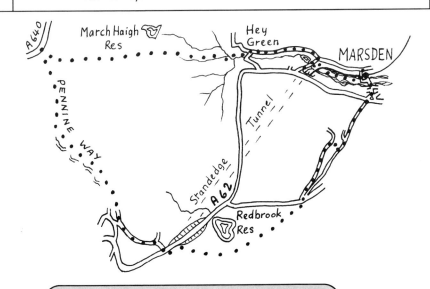

 6 miles.   3hours.

 Canal towpath, lanes, moorland paths and packhorse ways. This walk goes over some exposed areas and should only be tackled in good weather conditions and with protective clothing. Boots advised.

 Marsden town centre; Railway Inn by the station; coffee and snacks also available at the Tunnel End Canal and Countryside Centre.

 Pathfinder 702 Huddersfield and Marsden; 714 Holmfirth & Saddleworth Moor.

i *Marsden, in its cul-de-sac valley, developed as a staging post where travellers on foot and on horseback could pause before crossing the often perilous high Pennine watersheds between the West Riding and Cheshire or South Lancashire, utilising the many packhorse ways and steep moorland paths which can still be traced. It used to be said only half-jokingly that Marsden was the last place in the West Riding to discover the wheel.*

Marsden's history is closely connected with the Luddites. It was here that Enoch and James Taylor had their blacksmith's shop and began to manufacture the shearing frames that were to make many skilled croppers redundant, sparking the Luddite uprising. The Taylors also made huge sledge hammers which were nicknamed "Enochs", and used by the Luddites to smash machinery, hence the local saying "Enoch makes them and Enoch breaks them". The full story of the Luddites is told in the opening chapter.

ϰ From Marsden Station go up the steps which form the station exit, onto the railway bridge and turn left over the bridge. Where the road bends left towards the Railway Inn, take the track on the right which descends to a kissing gate into a small wooded picnic area on former railway sidings through a stile.

Keep on the path through the middle of the picnic area, but, where it ends in a small garden area, look for the steps on the right which take you down onto the towpath of the partly restored Huddersfield Narrow Canal. Turn left, continuing under the railway lines and pass the handsome Huddersfield Canal warehouse to a bridge over the canal. Cross and turn left past a small car park near Tunnel End.

i *Tunnel End is where the Narrow Canal disappears into the blackness of the famous Standedge Tunnel, the highest and longest canal tunnel in Britain, penetrating the Pennine bedrock for more than three miles.*

Much of the canal has already been restored, thanks to the initiatives of the Huddersfield Canal Society and several local authorities. There are ambitious plans to reopen the tunnel as a major tourist attraction. The former keeper's cottages at Tunnel End have been transformed into a delightful Canal and Countryside Centre, open most days of the year, with exhibitions of the canal and the area's rich heritage of transport and local history; there are also maps, local guidebooks and excellent coffee.

Return to the small car park and walk back up the lane, going left at the Tunnel End Inn and along Waters Road. You pass a disused and partly overgrown canal feeder reservoir and a row of

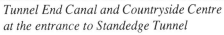 *Tunnel End Canal and Countryside Centre
at the entrance to Standedge Tunnel*

cottages to Hey Green, where, below the hotel entrance, there is a junction of lanes. Your way is directly ahead for a few metres, before bearing left along a signposted path through a metal pedestrian gate.

This leads along an attractive raised causeway above the infant River Colne, eventually emerging at Eastergate or Close Gate Bridge (SE 028 121).

i *This narrow, beautifully arched packhorse bridge carried the ancient trans-Pennine packhorse way , Rapes Highway, on its journey from Rochdale and Milnrow, in Lancashire, across to the Colne Valley of Yorkshire. At this point, on the left hand side of the two streams that meet, there used to be a packhorse inn. The pub was kept during the 18th century by one Esther Schofield whose name was corrupted to "Easter", the word "gate", dialect for road, now applied to the bridge, though the name Close Gate, as on the Ordnance Survey Map, is also sometimes used. Here the route enters the 5,685-acre Marsden Moor estate. Transferred to the National Trust in 1955, this vast sweep of unenclosed moorland contains evidence of the way transport has fashioned the landscape of the Colne Valley, from packhorse trails, Roman roads and canals to the Leeds-Liverpool railway. It also provides grazing for not a few sheep, too!*

The path follows the branching stream to the right for a few metres, before veering up a steep side valley to the left. The path climbs steadily up the ravine, and bears right once you reach the crest of the hill, dipping down into Willykay Clough, a narrow beck, before heading due west. Your clear route is along a narrow path over rough moor grass, now marked by a series of stone posts inscribed "PH Road".

i *These posts along Rapes Highway were erected by the local council after a legal dispute over its status as a public highway, early this century. Evidence at the court case came from people who had used the route in their childhood, including an eighty-year-old shepherd from Oldham, Sam Garside. He remembered leading his drunken father over the road at eleven o'clock at night, coming back from Marsden fair, with two hens in a basket and a tup (ram) following on behind.*

There are magnificent views on all sides across Oldgate Moor (its name comes from "the old road") looking back down the Colne Valley or ahead towards the hill, known as March Haigh, with its reservoir.

After about a mile, you will find yourself curving above and eventually down a shallow ravine, before swinging right to the A640 road, to meet the Pennine Way at a stream, Haigh Gutter, crossed by a footbridge (SE 003 123).

Go sharp left now, back across the beck and along the Pennine Way. This has been recently resurfaced, to protect it from erosion. The path bears slightly right to ascend Oldgate Moss, towards Northen Rotcher Crags.

As the route levels out you enjoy a fine, well-drained path along the edge of the moor, with truly magnificent views westwards across the industrial Lancashire plain, with still a few tall chimneys and big square brick mills to give a Lowryesque atmosphere.

You soon reach the memorial cairn (SE 005 112) to the Lancashire poet and topographer, Amon Wrigley (1861-1946), who wrote memorably about the Saddleworth area. Continue to the OS trig point before dropping down to the main A62 just before the narrow Standedge Cutting.

Cross the road, taking care with traffic, turn left and go up the path leaving the car park, following the Pennine Way signs. Follow the track round to the left, away from the Pennine Way, curving round above Redbrook Reservoir across open moor. The track descends slightly before it narrows to a path, crosses the beck (033 097) and climbs up to the road to Marsden. Cross the road, and take the left fork, Old Mount Road.

i *Old Mount Road is a surviving part of one of the earliest 18th century turnpike roads, built by Jack Metcalfe, "Blind Jack o' Knaresborough", the great road engineer, over Standedge, to carry mail coaches. This was well before the present A62 — a much later turnpike — was built to the north of Pule Hill in the 1820s.*

Where another stony track forks left again (SE038 103), take it, as it runs parallel to the Old Mount Road but keeps well above the field enclosures along the side of Pule Hill. As it bends right (SE042 108), take a walled path, forking more sharply to the right, marked by a National Trust sign. Drop by cottages to the left down to Old Mount Road. Turn left to descend into Marsden, crossing the main A62. Continue straight ahead for Marsden Church. Known as the "cathedral" of the Colne Valley, St Bartholmew's was built between 1894 and 1911. There are some interesting memorials in the graveyard, including a large granite obelisk to George Taylor Washington, so-called because he was born in America.

i *Opposite the church is a small park — the site of the old church. The first chapel was erected here in 1453, but was in such a poor condition that it was replaced in 1758. This church had an* *earthen floor so that worshippers could be buried within the church wall, a fact which was later to cause immense problems. This was exacerbated by the spread of Black Fever in 1798, which left 250 parishioners dead, forcing the church authorities to raise the graveyard artificially by three feet to accommodate all the corpses. The old church was finally demolished in 1896. The raised tomb of Enoch Taylor and other members of his family lies in the village green opposite.*

Not far from the church are the Old Stocks, mediaeval in origin and last used in 1821 when a character called Dutch Harry was locked up for six hours as a punishment for ringing the church bells late at night.

The Mechanics Institute, built in 1861, is one of the finest in Yorkshire, and on Warehouse Hill are to be seen a surviving row of tenterposts.

Turn left at the church, alongside of the River Colne and cross another lovely old packhorse bridge, Mellor Bridge, on the right. Turn left, but follow a narrow enclosed way ahead alongside a former mill, which ascends to emerge by the Railway Inn and the station.

Right: Castle Hill scene

Country walks from the Penistone Line

Beaumont Park and Blackwood Reservoir

Lockwood to Slaithwaite

This walk takes in an interesting mixture of features — one of the finest parks in Kirklees, woods, weavers' settlements and moorland tracks between deep Pennine valleys, whose mills add to the grandeur of the landscape.

 7 miles.

 4 hours.

Parkland, farm tracks and bridleways, some of which can be muddy after wet weather. The route ends with a series of field paths. Boots advisable.

Will o' Nats public house (5 miles); cafés, shops and pubs in Slaithwaite.

Pathfinder 702 Huddersfield and Marsden; Walk this Way – Deerhill and Blackmoorfoot Circle.

Break point:
Helme (4 miles). Bus 323 to Huddersfield (not Sundays).

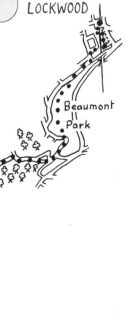

🕺   From Lockwood Station, the first stop on the Penistone line out of Huddersfield, take the exit steps to the main road. Cross directly ahead without going under the bridge, into a cul-de-sac, past K-Steels warehouse and parking bays. About 60 metres on the left is a concrete tunnel under the railway. Take this, turning right immediately beyond the railway into a track running alongside the railway and a woodyard. Follow it past bushes and street-ends; where it ends, turn right into Burbary Road, past Howarth's woodyard to an iron footbridge over the railway. Cross this bridge, keeping ahead to where it joins a street of Victorian houses. Turn left uphill to its junction with Moor End Road; go left again at the junction, then right up Beaumont Park Road for about 300 metres to where, on the left, a stone gateway leads into Beaumont Park. Turn right in the park, keeping on the higher track near the edge of the park.

🌿 *Beaumont Park occupies a steep hillside site overlooking the Lockwood Valley. There are panoramic views over the steep, wooded valley from several points, with Lockwood Viaduct on the Penistone Line a prominent feature. It is a typical handsome Victorian park, with several delightful features — a variety of pathways, shrubbery and exotic trees, rockeries, shelters, lawns, pavilions and formal gardens.*

Avoid the temptation, unless you have plenty of time, to explore the steep valley-side paths of the park, keeping to the broader path with benches, which runs along the top of the park, past the main entrance and alongside the fence by Beaumont Park Road. You pass toilets and the lodge, ignoring flights of steps out of the park or into a formal garden area ahead, keeping to the main path which bears to the left of the garden. Opposite an ornamental flight of twin stone steps on the right, take the track on the left, down steps through shrubbery and woods, which descends to the lower, southern entrance of the park, leading into Butternab Road, a deep side valley of the River Holme, known appropriately as Big Valley.

Cross to the pavement, right, and follow the road downhill, past the arches carrying the former Meltham railway line. But, where the road bends sharp left, go straight ahead and up a track ahead, bearing right over the former Meltham branch railway line and on up a cobbled lane. Keep straight ahead at a junction of tracks, following the cobbled track up past woodland and past a farm into Nether Moor Road, a narrow lane. Keep ahead for another 100 metres to the junction with a walled track (SE 121 135). Turn left here and go along the track past a farm, descending to a junction with another narrow lane. Follow this down to the valley bottom, crossing Dean Clough Beck before climbing to the junction with the lane from Blackmoorfoot. At the point where this lane goes round a tight bend, take the green track between walls on the right, going left at this track's junction with Turbid Lane, a slightly muddy farm track. Keep ahead at a junction to where this track bends right into Far Fields Lane, another long, narrow farm track between walls, well-used by cattle and therefore likely to be muddy — keep to the centre of the lane to avoid the worst of the mud.

Keep straight ahead where this enclosed track becomes a grassy way, going slightly left; where it ends (SE 108 120) take the main path diagonally left between fields, marked by gateposts, to Crosland Edge. This is a fine viewpoint, with Meltham below and Shooters' Nab to the right (SE 108 117).

The path continues over the wooden stile ahead to a farm track which descends steeply to a cottage; a linking path bears right just above the bracken by pylons; if you miss the turn, turn right uphill along the wall from the cottage (don't go through the stile at the cottage) to a stile in the wall some 80 metres above the cottage. This leads to a path below the wall to the farm ahead (SE 107 115). A stile in the wall corner leads into the farmyard; go through the pedestrian gate on the left, over a second stile, then head for the spire of Helme Church ahead, to locate stiles leading to the cross-roads below Helme. To avoid road walking, turn left for 150 metres to where a track, Hey Lane, leads to the hamlet of Hey, beyond which a Tarmac path goes towards Helme school. Bear right along a grassy path alongside the church wall to a stile. Cross the lane to a stile ahead, alongside the field to a track by a farm.

i *Note the row of weavers' cottages forming part of the farm-house on the left. Helme is a former weavers' settlement with several three-storey cottages, complete with lofts which once housed handlooms. Apart from a phone box, the village has no facilities but there are hourly buses (weekdays) to Meltham and Huddersfield (weekdays).*

Turn right, but where the track ends, a kissing gate by the gate on the left leads to a field path which bears left uphill over stiles, towards Orange Woods, an attractive oak wood. Keep straight ahead up to a ruined farm (SE 102 124); a stile on the left hand side of the garden wall leads to a path in front of the farm (on no account attempt to enter these buildings which are in a dangerous state); pass the old pumping station and walk across to the trees, keeping ahead of the grassy wall of the dam ahead, below which a path runs. Follow it to the right, towards small reservoir buildings and a stile into the road which runs along the dam wall. Turn left for about 20 metres to where a gap stile, marked with a yellow Walk this Way waymark, leads to a path along the water's edge. Continue to a picnic area and viewing point, at a small promontory by a shrubbery.

i *Blackmoorfoot Reservoir was built by Huddersfield Corpora-tion in 1876 and it still provides the town's main water sup-ply. A high level reservoir, it is also a haven for birdlife, especially during winter, when a variety of waders and waterfowl may be seen.*

Turn left immediately past the picnic area to a stile back to the dam-top road, going left again for about 50 metres to the second of two gap stiles in the stone wall, right opposite the wooden footpath signs. This leads to a path above and alongside the narrow feeder canal, or conduit. Follow this to the bridge which carries the main road over the conduit. Cross the bridge, but immediately turn left along the bridleway, Dunnock Road. Keep ahead around the hillside, Meltham Cop, enjoying splendid views across to Shooter's Nab and Meltham Moor. Turn right at the main road, Blackmoorfoot Road, and head for the pub, Will o' Nats, at a crossroads (SE 090 121).

ℹ *It was a little further along Blackmoorfoot Road that the Marsden mill owner, William Horsfall, was shot and fatally wounded by Luddite conspirators in 1812. Will o' Nats, a traditional moorland farmhouse-style building, takes its name from a former landlord, known as William, the son of Nathaniel. The pub, which sells food, is open daily, but closes at 3pm weekdays, 2.30pm Sundays.*

From Will o' Nats, take the broad, enclosed track directly opposite, which crosses Black Moor, now enclosed, giving views down to the reservoir to the right. Where this track meets the road, turn left for 25 metres to where a stile leads to a hillside path down to another stile in the lane below. The path continues down the hillside, over stiles and along a wall, keeping ahead to a gate, to the east of Lower Hey Farm (SE 085 133).

Steps above a gate lead down to an enclosed way; follow this downhill past another farm, but at the last field by a garage, before the path reaches modern housing, turn right through a stile waymarked with Colne Valley Walk signs, to Linfit Lane. Turn left down the lane but, at the housing estate turn, take the first left into Tudor Street; 50 metres on the right, between No. 14 and an electricity sub-station, a narrow, enclosed path leads past the backs of houses and gardens. At the bottom, turn right along the street, past houses. At the junction with Gordon Street is Linfit Fold and Linthwaite Hall.

ℹ *Linthwaite, or Linfit, Hall, is a late Elizabethan yeoman clothier's house, dating from about 1600, and typical of a prosperous clothier-farmer's house of the period, whose income was boosted by trade in locally produced cloth. The L-shaped building has several tall gables and mullioned windows, and a fine porch.*

Follow Gordon Street down to the busy Manchester Road and cross it. Immediately to the right of the bus shelter, take the narrow

Mills lining the canal at Slaithwaite

steps which lead down to a footbridge over the River Colne. Keep ahead to Waterside; turn right, following the lane into a mill complex before which, on the left, a path through what appears to be a small park is in fact Slaithwaite Canal Basin, a portion of the Huddersfield Narrow Canal, sadly filled in but making an attractive amenity area. Follow the Tarmac path between mill buildings to the centre of Slaithwaite. The road with a No Entry sign, sloping up past the Cooperative store, leads to the road and up to the railway station by the bridge on the right.

i *Slaithwaite, its name implying a Norse origin, grew around an ancient cruck house, known as Slaithwaite Hall, remnants of which survive near the present Tudor Manor House (Dartmouth Estate Office) in the town centre. This was the focal point of a township which consisted of several weaving hamlets and farmsteads. By mediaeval times small corn and fulling mills were established on side valleys. Industrialisation grew rapidly after the coming of the Huddersfield Narrow Canal in the 1790s, the wharves of what were known as Slawit Docks, being crowded with activity. Allegations of contraband being hidden in the canal to be redeemed at night-time, out of sight of customs officers, led to tales that*

Slawit men were merely trying to rake out the reflection of the moon in the canal when spotted at their activities. Hence was born the term "moonrakers" to describe local characters likely to be seen more often in the ale house than along the towpath. There was even a flourishing spa along the river at Slaithwaite in the early 19th century, with public baths, a concert hall, gardens and bowling greens.

The village, which expanded onto surrounding hillsides in the last and present centuries, has several attractive houses and mill buildings in its centre, and a church with a Venetian-style window and handsome tower which date from 1789, and no fewer than three inns. The railway station, closed by Beeching in 1968, was reopened by West Yorkshire PTE in 1982 and now enjoys a frequent train service to Manchester Victoria, Leeds and Wakefield.

Meltham and Wessenden

Honley to Marsden including the Kirklees Way

This walk links the Holme Valley with the Colne Valley through the
dramatic northern edge of the Peak National Park, contrasting
the gritstone oak woods of the Holme Valley with the open
moorland and wilder landscapes of the Dark Peak.

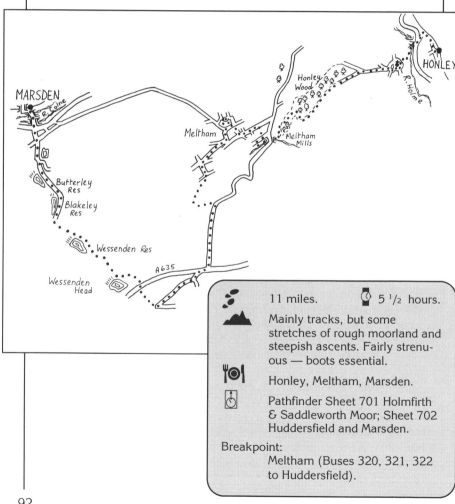

11 miles.   5 ½ hours.

Mainly tracks, but some
stretches of rough moorland and
steepish ascents. Fairly strenu-
ous — boots essential.

Honley, Meltham, Marsden.

Pathfinder Sheet 701 Holmfirth
& Saddleworth Moor; Sheet 702
Huddersfield and Marsden.

Breakpoint:
Meltham (Buses 320, 321, 322
to Huddersfield).

🏃 As you leave Honley Station's single platform down the steps to the entrance, turn sharp right towards a small industrial depot with locked gates, immediately to the left of which (and invisible till you reach it) is a gap stile and footpath leading to an enclosed footpath by the railway and alongside the depot, a hedge and gardens. Keep walking straight ahead to the road, crossing it and continuing in the same direction as the path now becomes a broader access drive. Where this swings right, keep ahead on a narrow path, still alongside the railway. The path soon drops down a long flight of stone steps, through woods, to join the path coming from under the railway tunnel (SE 143 128). Keep left to join a lane on the embankment, leading to the main road. Cross this fast and busy road carefully.

Take the first lane right by the Suncharm soft drinks factory, crossing the bridge; don't go uphill, but take the first track left past houses, which leads into a footpath going over a footbridge over Mag Brook. Cross, keeping along and above the River Holme. As you reach another row of houses ahead, take the stone stile on the right into a paved way alongside the end of the houses, climbing up to a courtyard and Honley Church.

ℹ️ *Honley is an attractive, compact village situated on the summit of a small hill. Its church, with its narrow, elegant tower, dates from 1843, and makes a notable landmark in the Colne Valley. It is worth spending a few minutes exploring the town and discovering some delightful examples of weavers' cottages, hidden in small folds and courtyards.*

Turn right at the church but then take the first road left, School Street, past cottages and the village school, turning right at the end by the Liberal Club, to Town Head. Take the narrow cobbled street on the left, Berry Croft, walking steeply downhill past Honley Silver Band's rooms. Where the street bends sharply to the right, continue down the steps in the wall corner down to the crossroads below.

Cross the road, and turn left for a short distance to a junction where another lane, Scotgate Road, bears off right, climbing past cottages, a small factory and eventually past a junction and a line of new houses, for a distance of almost half a mile to where, at the top of the hill, the road levels out at a wood and bears right at a junction. At this point a track, Scotgate, bears slightly left. Take this way.

This track soon thins out to become a beautiful footpath running along the edge of a Honley Old Wood — at first this is dense oak and birch, but beyond the quarry and cottages and a barrier, the trees thin out to reveal patches of attractive heather among scattered birch. Keep straight ahead for about a mile before the path squeezes between the stone wall and field to the left, and the fence of a former quarry, now a tip, to the right. Keep walking in the same

Typical Pennine woodland scene (Honley Woods)

direction past the quarry entrance, the path continuing in the same
direction before descending in a series of zigzags to emerge at
Meltham Mills alongside long factory sheds. This is the former site
of the world-famous David Brown tractor company, now containing
industrial workshops.

Turn right downhill. At the bottom of the hill is a little park.
Enter the park, and follow its main path to the left, past a small
playground, benches, shrubbery and a waterfall. Where you reach
a metal footbridge on the right, opposite terraced houses, cross
over this bridge keeping straight ahead past the gable end of
houses, to bear right up steps to the lane, Mill Bank Road. Turn
right by mill cottages and continue for 200 metres, looking for
where an unsigned alleyway with handrails, known as Roods Path,
climbs past the gardens of new houses. Follow it over the brow of
the hill; the path soon descends to join the main Huddersfield road
by lodge gates. Turn left, past more suburban houses, for about
300 metres to where a short street, Near Lane, opposite car
showrooms, leads to a footpath. Where it bears left, continue
straight ahead across a curved iron footbridge with a fine view of
the old station site, before crossing the valley floor and ascending
up steps to reach Mean Lane.

i *The former branch of the Lancashire & Yorkshire Railway came to Meltham in 1869, serving the town for more than 80 years before submitting to road competition and closing to passengers in 1949 and to freight in 1965. In its heyday there were a dozen commuter trains a day from Huddersfield.*

Cross the road and turn left here, but at the handsome Meltham Baptist Chapel ahead, bear right behind the chapel to locate a flagged path by the graveyard. This leads into a cobbled, enclosed path; follow it to the right, beside allotments, until it reaches Broadlands Road and a housing estate. Turn left past garages, bearing left at the junction. There are superb views across Meltham town from here. Look for a narrow concrete path with a handrail on the left, by the allotments. Take this down to a narrow estate road, where, after a few metres on the right, steps continue to the road between cottages where you cross to an open green by the beck and its waterfalls. Turn left downhill and right into Station Road, to the centre of Meltham and Meltham Church.

i *Meltham is a typical Pennine mill town, dominated by moor-land scenery and its handsome stone textile and engineering mills. Most of the town is Victorian, with a choice of pubs, cafés and shops around the town centre crossroads (coffee shop by post office), and there is a handsome Georgian Parish Church dating from 1786. Its bell tower was added in 1835. The Baptist Chapel, founded in 1816 and rebuilt in 1864, is on a suitably grand scale and indicates the strong influence of the nonconformist tradition in the town. There are frequent buses back to Huddersfield should you decide to terminate the walk here.*

Immediately past the church, turn right into Green End Road. Follow it around to the right, to its junction with Colders Lane. Turn left up Colders Lane, passing a mixture of bungalows and old cottages, soon climbing uphill to where the road thins out and ends, continuing as a narrow packhorse way, climbing between the fields and below a farm. At Rose Cottage (SE 093102) it meets a broader track. Turn left. Cross the main Wessenden Head road and continue along the track, Langroyd Lane, climbing uphill over a catchwater drain up to Royd Edge, a fine viewpoint across the intimate valley of Royd End Clough. Here the path emerges above a heather-covered hillside. Nearby, a typical small Pennine mill, also known as Royd Edge, nestles in the valley bottom.

Turn right, past the former Royd Edge Quarries, but at the fork, follow the track on the left down to Sun Royd Farm (SE 091 094). You are now in the Peak National Park, and as you reach the farm look for the Peak Park waymarks and signs at a stile, left, taking you across the corner of the field to another stile. From here follow the wall then the waymark posts down to cross the stream (tricky after very wet weather), picking up a faint line of green path through marshy ground which swings up and curves sharply to the right, becoming more distinct as it heads between gate posts and uphill to the ruined Royd Farm. Keep straight ahead now and uphill, avoiding waterlogged areas by keeping to the edge of the track on the right, climbing up to join a broader and drier track at a gate.

Turn right into this track, Magdalen Road. Soon past Ash Royd Farm it becomes a steep, grassy path climbing along the edge of Meltham Moor, with impressive views to the right across Rams Clough. Follow this way for almost a mile to the crest of the hill and another gate, beyond which is the main road Greenfield-Holmfirth road (A635).

Turn right for 100 metres to where, on the left, a gate and stile lead to a descending track with curious twin-hollowed causeway stones, probably serving an old sandstone quarry, soon passed on the right. Keep straight ahead over a ladder stile at the junction with Nether Lane, a track climbing up from Digley Reservoir, waymarked with the Kirklees Way blue circles. The Kirklees Way will now lead you to Marsden Station. This track edges around the northern rim of a beech wood, crossing a moorland stream by a primitive footbridge and ascending above Reap Clough. As the path levels out by a wall (SE 079 070), turn right to head up the hillside alongside the wall, cutting off the corner to a ladder stile over the retaining wall at the road.

ℹ️ The gatepost and ruins on the left mark the site of the Isle of Skye Inn. This was a popular coaching inn which stood near this lonely crossroads to serve travellers on the Holmfirth-Greenfield turnpike road across the moors, which was built in 1822. For many years, it was a favourite refreshment stop where you could enjoy a pot of tea or a pint of ale with your own sandwiches. It was equally popular with walkers, cyclists and motorists, but was demolished in the early 1960s, largely because it was seen to be a source of pollution of the surrounding moorland water-gathering grounds.

Cross the main A635 to the junction with the Meltham road, right, following this lane (Kirklees Way waymark), as it ascends and curves for about a quarter of a mile to where, at a barrier, a track on the left leads gently downhill through the valley.

ℹ️ This is a famous track through the Wessenden Valley in the Peak National Park, past a series of four linked reservoirs — Wessenden Head, Old Wessenden, Blakeley and Butterley. Most of this valley, which has much of the austere beauty of the Scottish Highlands, lies within the National Trust's Marsden Moor estate. A loop on the 270-mile long Pennine

Way, Britain's most popular National Trail, joins this track down into Marsden.

Follow the narrow track down past Lazing Clough and around the long loop around Sike Clough before reaching Wessenden Lodge, an isolated farm and another former tea room. Before this the track bears left below the farm and joins a broader access path, soon reaching Blakeley and Butterley reservoirs as the rooftops and steep streets of Marsden come into view. Past Butterley Reservoir the track joins a steep street. Keep straight ahead, past terrace houses into the town centre, by a small roundabout, continuing past a massive mill complex and underneath the flyover carrying Manchester Road (A62) past the centre of Marsden — the Luddite town.

Keep straight ahead, past the church and village green, with its stocks and the tomb of Enoch Taylor, turning left along the road, past the church to Mellor Bridge, the packhorse bridge at Clough Lee, over the River Colne. Keep left to the mill, but bear right up a steep narrow path, at the top of which is the road past the Huddersfield Canal locks, leading to the platforms of Marsden Station (access by steps from the road bridge) ahead, and the Railway Inn on the right if there's time before your train.

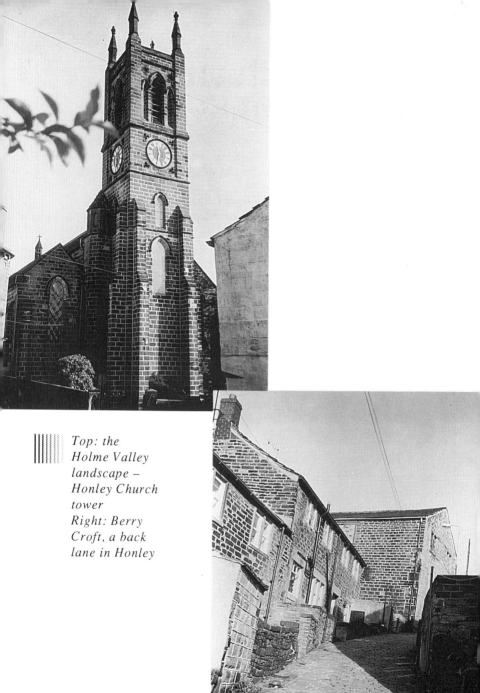

Top: the Holme Valley landscape – Honley Church tower
Right: Berry Croft, a back lane in Honley

Holmfirth and the Lower Holme Valley

Brockholes to Honley

The Lower Holme Valley is a delightful mix of weaving hamlets and early industrial millscapes. This walk explores Holmfirth and villages of the Holme Valley which provide the backdrop to the adventures of Compo, Foggy and Clegg in the TV series Last of the Summer Wine.

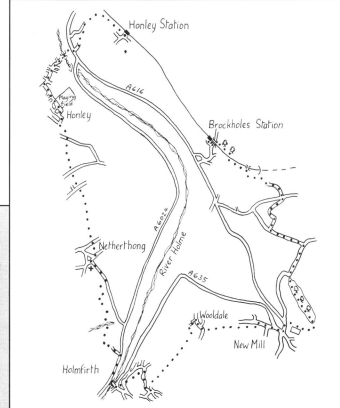

 9 miles.

5¹/₂ hours.

Mainly field paths and bridleways, some of which can be fairly muddy in wet weather. Boots recommended.

 Pubs in New Mill and Wooldale; cafés, shops and pubs in Holmfirth and Honley.

 Pathfinders 702 Huddersfield and Marsden, 714 Holmfirth and Saddleworth Moor; Walk this Way – 'Villages and Views', 'Castle Hill and Honley Station'.

🚶 From Brockholes Railway Station, turn left up the road and go under the railway bridge. Immediately on the right is an attractive path through oak woodland. Follow the path back under the railway and along a fence to an old stone kissing gate and a railway bridge. At the bridge turn right through the woods and continue straight ahead across fields to a line of three gates and a stile. Go over the stile to follow a green lane which gradually becomes cobbled and emerges at a Tarmac lane and a group of old farm houses. Continue along the lane to the road.

Turn left up the road and then take the first sharp right along a lane lined by a row of cottages. The lane bends left and becomes a muddy track. Follow this track along the edge of the hillside. On the left is a small quarry and, on the right, views across the lower Holme Valley. Continue to a gap stile and begin to descend the path lined with gorse bushes to a gate and lane. Turn left along the lane to join a road. Walk along the road past a group of fine Scots Pines and over the brow of the hill. As the road begins to descend, look for a gate and muddy track on the left. Go through the stile by the edge of the gate.

Over the stile, walk along the track to some holly bushes and look for a small path on the right. The path follows the wall to a stone stile. Over the stile, continue straight ahead, descending the hill to a wooden stile and woodland. From here there are magnificent views down into New Mill and the huge complex of Moorbrook mills, with its chimney and rows of weaving sheds. Walk through woods and follow the path down the edge of field to the houses below and a lane (Coal Pit Lane). Turn right down the lane to the road and the centre of New Mill.

Sid's – the classic Yorkshire café – formerly an ironmonger's

🛈 *New Mill is an attractive village which, as its name suggests, was once the site of the manorial mill. In 1780 the first scribbling engine for carding wool was built here, heralding the beginning of the industrial revolution in woollen textile production in the Holme Valley.*

Cross the road and turn right past the 15th century Maythorne Cross which stands outside the local library; at the road junction turn left. At a small car park, cross the road and turn left up Greenhill Bank Road which climbs up a hillside, past Moorbrook mills. Turn right along Royds Avenue and past a group of houses. Look for a clear green space on the right and walk towards the fence. Turn right and then follow a path along the edge of the recreation ground, towards a small playground. At the playground, walk down to the houses in the far corner, towards a small gap alongside the end house. Keep straight ahead, ignoring the path on the right by the garages, but continue through the woods along a faint path. Follow the path across a stream and then uphill past the remains of old greenhouses to a join a cobbled track leading into Wooldale.

i *Old Wooldale has some of the oldest and most interesting buildings in the valley. Its development was influenced by the Quaker, Henry Jackson, who was one of the principal founders of the Wooldale Friends' Meeting House. This is one of the earliest Quaker meeting houses in the country and was built before the Act of Toleration (in 1689) which allowed the Friends to worship openly.*

Turn right into Wooldale and take the first left, South Street. The lane swings sharp right, passing the old post office on the left, and joins a green lane. Follow this lane for about half a mile. To the left are views back down into New Mill. The lane appears to end abruptly at a wall. Turn right through the gap in the wall and continue in the same direction as before, keeping the wall on the left. At the end of the field, go through the gap in the wall to a sandy track and turn left onto the road. At the road turn right, following the road past a group of weavers' cottages on the right. Just past Redvers House, turn sharp left down a lane.

From here there are some magnificent views down into Holmfirth, with its steeply stepped terraces of weavers' cottages and groups of mills huddled in the valley bottom.

Go down the steps and follow a series of clear ginnels down to a lane. Turn left to Bunkers Hill and walk down towards the back of the Parish Church. Go down the steps at the side of the church past Sid's Café, into Holmfirth.

Holmfirth is a delightful bustling town full of intriguing alleyways and courtyards. For devotees of Last of the Summer Wine, there is also the chance to see Nora Batty's house, sample a pot of tea at Sid's Café, and indulge in a little nostalgia in the Last of the Summer Wine Exhibition. A history and more detailed description of Holmfirth is provided in the Holmfirth Town Walk.

From Sid's Café, cross the main road and turn left to the bridge. Cross the River Holme and continue up Victoria Street to the traffic lights. Turn right and go past the Civic Hall and Postcard Pub. Just before the Institute of Adult Education, built in 1894, is a steep lane on the right. The lane continues past some houses and soon becomes a green track. Towards the summit is a conveniently sited bench from where you can enjoy views down into Holmfirth and across the valley to the sandstone cliffs above the town. At the bench, turn right and continue along the lane which swings left to follow an attractive valley. The lane descends to a stream; cross the stream and go through the bridle gate straight ahead and continue along an enclosed track. The track swings right to join a lane which leads into Netherthong.

Netherthong is an attractive weaving settlement. You can still see the three-storey cottages with their long rows of mullioned windows. Some houses still have the remains of the taking-in doors at the top of the building, used to bring in the raw wool and take out the finished cloth. All Saints Church is a Commissioners', or Waterloo Church, and was built in 1829. The Lord Commissioner for the Treasury administered a fund of £1 million for the building of churches in new areas as a thanksgiving for the victory against Napoleon at the Battle of Waterloo.

At the church, cross the road towards the war memorial and follow the road straight ahead past the Clothiers' Arms. Just past the Victorian school take the cobbled ginnel on the left, down to a bridge overlooked by a row of weavers' cottages. Continue over the bridge, past the Cricketers' Arms. Go through a white gate by the side of a house and walk towards a stile. Go over the stile and follow the line of the wall through a gateway. Cross the field and then walk straight up the hill, following the wall. At the top of the field turn right to a gap stile which leads to a field and a second stone stile.

From here you can see the 1,000ft Emley Moor television transmitter mast and Victoria Tower on Castle Hill, as well as enjoy-

ing views down into Honley and Huddersfield.

A clear field path leads to a track, cross the track to a stile and follow the path to a road. Cross the road. Almost opposite is a signed footpath by some houses, which leads through fields to a second road. Cross the road and turn left. Just opposite a bench by a bus stop is a small stone stile. Go over the stile and walk diagonally across the field towards some new houses. At the house, turn left along an enclosed path which leads down to the road. Follow the road to the Honley Community Centre and then turn right to follow an alleyway which runs along the far side of the building to a road. Cross the road and take the steps opposite and follow a paved path to a road. Cross the road and turn left along a playing field wall to a gap. Turn right through the gap, following a path along the edge of the playing fields and past an old toilet block, to some houses. At the houses turn left along a path and continue, ignoring a lane veering off to the right, to some sheds. The path runs between the sheds towards a group of bollards before joining a lane which leads into Honley's main street, Westgate, opposite the post office.

ℹ *Honley is an attractive village, with interesting alleyways and charming folds of weavers' cottages, which is well worth taking the time to explore. Bear in mind, however, that the station is about half an hour's walk from the town. In the churchyard of St Mary's are the old village stocks. The Coach and Horses Inn has strong Luddite connections — it was here, in 1812, that Benjamin Walker and Thomas Smith, two Luddites, spent the night drinking after murdering the Marsden mill owner, William Horsfall (see page 18). The landlady was afterwards called to give evidence at their trial in York.*

Turn right down Westgate, to the Coach and Horses Inn, past an interesting well, dated 1796, whose date stone informs passers by they will be fined 10 shillings for defouling the water. At the Coach and Horses, take the footpath on the left, following the riverside through Honley Woods. Cross the white footbridge and continue alongside the river to some mill cottages. Cross the river by a second white bridge past the Ben Shaws and Suncharm soft drinks factory, to the main road. Cross this road with care and then turn left up a minor road which leads up a wooded hillside. Take the track on the right, part of the Walk this Way route to Castlehill from Honley Station, and just before the tunnel under the railway, take the flight of steps to the right through the woods. The path continues at the top of the steps, alongside the railway line, crossing a road and taking you along the ginnel opposite, before finally emerging at a cobbled lane by Honley Railway Station.

Over page: view across Royd House' woods towards Castle Hill

Farnley Tyas and Castle Hill

Stocksmoor to Berry Brow

This is a walk dominated by woodland, lanes, fields and unspoiled countryside in south Kirklees, to Castle Hill, which offers one of the finest viewpoints in the South Pennines.

🐾	6 miles.	⌚	3¹/₂ hours.

⛰️ Lanes, field paths and woodland. Some muddy sections, so boots advised. Moderate in difficulty.

🍴 Public houses at Stocksmoor (Clothier's Arms), Farnley Tyas and Castle Hill (allow an hour for the walk from Castle Hill).

🧭 Pathfinder Sheet 702 Huddersfield and Marsden; Walk this Way – Castlehill and Honley Station.

Breakpoint:
Farnley Tyas (4 miles); Bus 340 to Huddersfield.

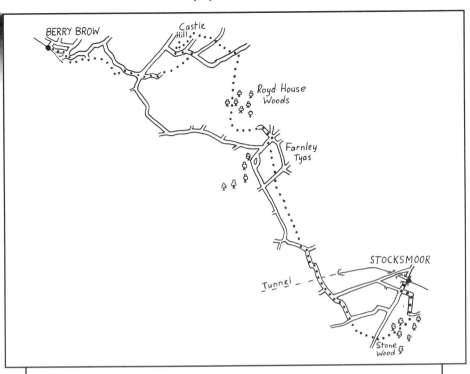

Man's mark on the horizon — Emley Moor Television Mast

🚶 From Stocksmoor Station entrance, turn left into Station Road and pass modern housing to the first turning on the left, Shepley Road, some 200 metres from the station. Where the pavement ends, keep to the right hand side of this quiet lane as it descends to meet Stone Wood at a bridge over Stone Wood Dike (SE 184104).

Take the path through the kissing gate on the right into Stone Wood. The path climbs through this lovely birch, beech and holly wood, away from the stream, before eventually descending back to the streamside. Close to the end of the wood, ford the stream at stepping stones. Continue to the stile by the bridge carrying Fulstone Road. The path continues directly opposite by trees, to a stile and then by a hedge and a fence along the edge of a long field. There are fine views across rolling countryside towards Emley Moor Television mast.

At the top of the field you emerge at a crossroads (SE 176 104). Take the narrow lane on the right, Ing Head Lane, keeping to the right to face traffic, soon passing Ing Head Farm, now kennels. Keep ahead to the crossroads with Stocks Road, and where this bends left past the bus stops, continue ahead, following the Farnley Tyas sign, along Brown's Knoll Road, past Moor Bottom Farm, with fine views across to the village of Thurstonland and its distinctive church, on the left.

At the junction with Green Side Road, turn left for 200 metres to where, on the right, you'll see a signed path indicating a stile with steep steps (SE 168 114). Now cross the broad field in the same direction, heading for a tree, to the left of which, by a stump, is the next stile. The path, well used and therefore fairly clear on the ground, now follows the field edge.

ᔰ *At this point you are following a long, low ridge above the Holme Valley. There are open views from here across to Kirkburton and the little Fenay Valley, east of Huddersfield, as well as to the foothills of the Dark Peak to the south. Note the unusual brick crenelated building on the right, a Victorian water tower.*

The path crosses two more stiles before bearing slightly left over a field to a stile in the field centre, continuing along the edge of the next field over more stiles, and across a track. The little tower of Farnley Tyas Church makes a natural orientation point ahead. Cross more stiles below a large house, Whinny Wood Farm, bearing slightly right eventually to cross to a stone stile a few metres to the right of a field gate, and into a lane (SE 165 123). Turn right. Almost immediately, on the left, a stile by a field gate gives access to another path by a wall; head for a gate, by the side of which a stile leads into an enclosed, but rather muddy track, which emerges in Farnley Tyas, between the farm and the village's little, early Victorian church, dedicated to St Lucius (1838-40). Turn right into the village centre and the crossroads, with the Golden Cock pub, which is more than 400 years old.

🛈 *Farnley Tyas is a particularly attractive agricultural village, amazingly rural, considering it is less than three miles from the centre of Huddersfield, with scattered stone farms and barns, some of them converted to houses, and 18th and 19th century workers' cottages, grouped around the crossroads. It is an ancient settlement and mentioned in the Domesday book of 1086 as "Fereleia". Tyas derives from the le Teyeis family who held much of the land in the neighbourhood from the 13th century.*

Turn immediately left past the Golden Cock, but then take the first track on the left, Cliffe Lane. Follow this downhill into a shallow valley with the long ridge, including Castle Hill and its tower, dominating the skyline directly ahead. Keep along the lane as it bends to the left, but where it ends, at the fork of two waymarked paths, take the lower path, to the right, which swings down the hillside to enter Royd House Woods at a stile (SE 162 131).

Descend through these lovely beech, sycamore, and oak woods, along a clear and waymarked path which crosses streamlets by a series by stone slabs. Stiles lead across a small clearing into the wood once again, before finally leaving the wood across a pasture. The path, less distinct, cuts across the corner of a field to the wood ahead where, to the right of a field gate, you'll see a waymarked post by a broad gap in a wall, leading into the wood.

Take this path, keeping straight ahead through the centre of the wood to a stile with triple waymarks. Take the centre path straight ahead, descending steps to a stream, crossed by footbridge and stepping stones. Climb up steps to the stile ahead and continue alongside a field to a gateway in the hedge above. Turn right here, following the waymark, keeping the hedge on the left. But, where the hedge ends, turn left across the field up to a gate, into Lumb Lane, by a bench (SE 158 138). Cross and turn left to another stile and a signed path on the right, which leads up a field alongside a stream. Where wooden pylons cross overhead, go right through the holly bushes into a narrow enclosed green way, which bears left, uphill between old thorn hedges. Turn right at the drive to the summit of Castle Hill, but at the sharp bend, take the sandy steps on the left, which lead to a path with panoramic views. It curves around the summit, along old earthworks, with views down into the Colne Valley ahead, and across to the high Pennine summits, Pule Hill and beyond. At the concrete steps, turn right up to the tower and pub.

ℹ *Castle Hill is a 900ft landmark dominating the Huddersfield area and providing views across the Pennines, Huddersfield and outlying suburbs. Castle Hill is shrouded in legend, including one that claims that treasure is buried beneath the hill and others that talk of a network of tunnels linking nearby villages. More exotic tales hint at dragons and devils leaping through the air. For all that, Castle Hill is of major archaeological importance. Excavations have revealed that the site was first occupied 4,000 years ago by Neolithic settlers from Europe who built simple earth ramparts to defend the site. Flint tools found at the site are now in the Tolson Museum in Huddersfield.*

Castle Hill was later developed as an Iron Age fort around 555 BC. According to legend, the Celtic Queen Cartimandua, Queen of the Brigantes, used Castle Hill as a base during the Roman occupation. More than 1,500 years later, in 1147 AD, the Normans built a large motte and bailey castle and restored many of the original earthworks by constructing a large ditch and rampart on the western side of the hill. In later years the castle was used as a hunting lodge, and finally demolished in the 14th century.

It was on Castle Hill that a beacon was lit to warn of the approach of the Spanish Armada, and another prepared in case of an invasion by Napoleon. Castle Hill's prominent position also made it a popular venue in the 18th and 19th centuries for prize fighting, dog fighting and illegal cockfights. The Castle Tavern was built in 1812, but the present building dates from the 1850s. Jubilee Tower was built in 1899 to celebrate Queen Victoria's Diamond Jubilee. It is open on summer weekends, when visitors can climb the 165 steps to admire the view from the top.

Return to descend the steps to the drive, turning left for some 300 metres down to the long white farmhouse, just before which a waymarked path leads alongside a wall, by fields, eventually entering a walled green track to Castle Houses Farm. Turn right through the farmyard and along a short access road, past cottages into Ashes Lane. Turn right here for a few metres, before turning left into a track; but where this forks, take the lower grassy track to the right, down to Cold Hill Farm (SE 145 137). Just before the first house on the left look for a stone stile on the left, by the wall. The path follows the garden wall to the right into a narrow lane. Follow it downhill, but where its opens out into a field, keep alongside the hedge on the right at the top of the field to a gap stile in the corner.

Cross this field, descending towards the tall blocks of flats ahead, veering half left, past holly bushes and heading for the field corner to a gap stile. Keep to the well-marked path to the left of the stone wall, which descends to the playing field by the railway line, with fine views of the great mill complex around Armitage Bridge. Turn right, around the edge of the soccer pitch to the wall at the far side where you'll find a gap stile leading to Lady House Lane. Turn left to the junction into Bridge Street close to the railway bridge, but then go right, uphill into Newsome Road, towards the bus stop on the corner of Birch Road. Turn left here, past Berry Brow Junior School, heading for the large red Metro sign 200 metres ahead where, on the left, you'll find the sloping entrance down to the attractive new Berry Brow Station halt (SE 137139), its shelter and single platform surrounded by a carefully planted shrub garden.

Upper Denby and Penistone

Shepley to Penistone

A walk exploring some of the old packhorse ways, bridleways and footpaths around Denby Dale on the borders of West and South Yorkshire.

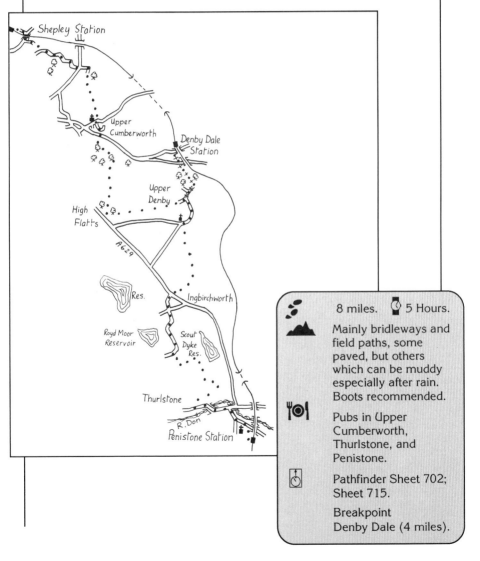

8 miles. 5 Hours.

Mainly bridleways and field paths, some paved, but others which can be muddy especially after rain. Boots recommended.

Pubs in Upper Cumberworth, Thurlstone, and Penistone.

Pathfinder Sheet 702; Sheet 715.

Breakpoint Denby Dale (4 miles).

⚐ Walk down the track from Shepley Station to the road, and turn right under the railway bridge. Take the lane immediately on the left, which winds it way up to a group of houses. As the lane bends to the right take the bridleway on the left signed with a blue "K" — the Kirklees Way. This is an attractive lane, lined with hedgerows, which descends through woodland. The path crosses a small bridge and leads to a road. Cross the road and take the track opposite, past the farm house on the left. Where the track bends steeply to the right, continue straight ahead to a stile in the wall, leading into woodland. Go up the steps and turn right, following the line of the stream through the beech trees. The path emerges into fields via a stile. Follow the edge of the field to a second stile and head up the hill towards Upper Cumberworth. A stile in the corner of the field leads onto a lane. Walk straight ahead towards the Church.

ℹ *Upper Cumberworth is an old settlement with an interesting church, St Nicholas's. In the churchyard are the old village stocks.*

Turn right and walk along the road, turning left down Hollybank Avenue. Continue past modern housing; the footpath is clearly signed at the bottom of the hill, between houses. The path leads down to the main road; cross the road and almost opposite is a delightful narrow enclosed path which leads into a small wooded valley. As the path enters the woods, turn left, to follow the wall which emerges at a track. Turn right down to the stream and an unusual small ford with a conveniently placed handrail. Cross the ford and bear left through the woods and rhododendron shrubs. At the clearing marked by a large group of stones, the path forks. Take the left fork which emerges at a tiny bridge and a stile leading onto a track.

Turn right down the track to a bridge and a series of stone steps leading up to a stile. Through the stile, continue up the field straight ahead, avoiding the temptation to follow the clearer path on the left. At the wall look for a stile. Go over the stile and continue through the next field to a stile by a gate. Through the stile veer right, following the line of a small brook on the left. Climb up a short hill towards a group of trees and a wall. A large holly bush marks the stile and the right of way. Turn left and follow the path through the trees to a lane. At the lane turn right into High Flats.

☀ *From here is a splendid view back across two small reservoirs to the valley below.*

At the lane junction, turn left past the Quaker cemetery, with its simple gravestones, bearing simply the names of the deceased and the dates they lived.

ℹ *High Flats is 976ft above the valley and this remote spot was deliberately chosen by a group of Quakers in the 1660s to found* *a settlement in which they could practise their faith without fear of persecution. Quakerism began as a movement against organised religion, "steeplehouse" worship and the "hirling ministry". Supporters renounced the creed, sacraments, paid ministry, the taking of oaths and payment of tithes, and instead laid emphasis on the individual's own personal inward relationship with God. The Quakers originally met in a barn but, after the Act of Toleration in 1689, built this meeting house in 1726 on the site of the barn. Members of the community were mostly involved in cloth production and farming. A converted barn opposite the meeting house was once a boarding school for Quaker boys and, on its far gable, is a sundial which reads "Labor et spe".*

At the barn, turn right and look for a kissing gate on the left. Follow the narrow enclosed path down to a stream and up some steps, alongside the edge of field to a stile and a muddy lane. Turn right and, almost immediately, go through a stile on the left. Follow the field wall to a second stile and turn right and walk towards a house and lane.

Go through the stile by the side of the iron lamp post and continue along a field path to a lane. From here there are magnificent views over to Emley TV mast. Continue straight ahead over the rather dilapidated stone stile in the field corner and follow the field path to a muddy lane. Walk along the lane to a junction. To continue the walk, turn right into Upper Denby.

If you wish to finish the walk at Denby Dale, turn left and, at the next junction of paths, follow the signed public bridleway down into Denby Dale, which meanders through attractive woodland. Where the path meets the road, cross over and take the footpath opposite which runs along the foot of the Denby Dale viaduct to emerge at the main road near the station. Cross the road and walk under the viaduct and take the path on the left up to the station.

i *Upper Denby is a pleasant hamlet whose church, St John, once served the entire valley. Denby was a Chaplaincy within the Parish of Penistone and, prior to 1627, when a Chapel of Ease was built, parishioners had to walk to Penistone to worship. By 1839 Bishop Longley found the church "in a miserable, filthy and ruinous state" and ordered its demolition. The 17th century tower was retained and the present building dates from 1842-3. A chancel was added in 1900 under the direction of the then incumbent, Romeo Taglis.*

At the main road turn right. Just before the church, turn left to where a bridleway, signed Ingbirchworth, branches off left through a small gate. Bear left between a barbed wire fence and a wall, to a gate. Continue along a narrow path following a stream, before descending into a delightful wooden valley. Cross a bridge to a gate and, keeping the hedge on the left, follow the waymarked field path. Where the path crosses a muddy track, turn right towards a farm, following a wooden fence. Look for a wooden stile on the left; go over the stile and walk diagonally across the field towards a white gate and a stone stile in the corner. Continue across a narrow field and turn right at the road. Go down Mill Lane to a stream. Turn left along the road at Cherry Tree Cottage.

As the road swings left at a elegantly converted barn, turn left up a track and then right along an enclosed track between a house and a barn. Follow the bridleway until it emerges at a road. Continue straight ahead, ignoring the first public footpath on the left but take the second along a track to a field. Turn right and bear slightly right, towards the field wall. Follow the wall down to a stile in the corner of a field. Walk along the edge of the field and up the track to a group of houses. Turn left and follow the track to the road and turn right into Thurlstone.

i Thurlstone is a pleasing mixture of old and new, with some particularly attractive gritstone weavers' cottages. Thurlstone was known for its white cloth, called Penistones, woven from the wool of locally bred sheep. Nicholas Saunderson, the blind Cambridge Professor of Mathematics, was born here in 1682. Blinded by smallpox at the age of two, he taught himself to read by passing his fingers over the carved gravestones in Penistone churchyard. An inscribed stone from the house where he was born is set in a wall in the centre of the village.

Take the turning first left and walk along a lane. Just past a house (1793) that looks as if it was once a chapel, go through the stone stile on the right and walk diagonally across the field to a gate. Go through the gate and take the path on the right to the lane and River Don, and turn right to the main road. At the road turn sharp left over the bridge, then take the next lane on the right, Stottercliffe Road, before turning left to follow a bridleway. Ignore the path along the old railway line but take an enclosed path which cuts through some trees to playing fields. Walk straight ahead towards the fire station. At the lane continue straight ahead through the Cattle Market into Penistone.

i Penistone is one of the highest market towns in the country, having been sited on one of the main trading routes across the Pennines in the early days of the textile industry. It was once an important centre and, among buildings of interest, are a rare 17th century Dissenters' Chapel, an 18th century cloth hall and an interesting 15th century church in which the ancestors of the poet William Wordsworth are buried.

Allow at least ten minutes to get to the station. Go down Church Street to the left of the church and under the railway bridge at the bottom of the hill. Immediately on the right is the drive to the railway station.